Praise for *Danger Music*

'I was deeply moved by this book. I was moved by the plight of the children living through this hell and moved by their bravery and that of their families. And I was moved by Eddie's decision to finally find the courage to become the man he always knew he was.' *Good Reading*

'*Danger Music* moves in whirlwind snippets through Eddie's days teaching in Kabul. Students appear and disappear with startling irregularity . . . The stress, uncertainty and trauma of everyday life in Kabul are felt keenly in this whirlwind narrative. In one moment, Eddie is describing the beauty of the young cello players playing together; in another, he's wondering how to get everyone out if suicide bombers and the Taliban storm the school. I loved this book.' Readings

'Never upstaging his students' dramas even as he struggles with his own identity, Eddie Ayres writes with forthrightness and compassion in this timely, powerfully-told tale.' *The Age*

'Eddie shares his brave journey to self-knowledge and self-acceptance and opens our eyes to the beauty that can be found in the worst of places. It is a brave and incredibly inspiring story.' *OUTinPerth*

'The book is so immersive, that the reader feels a sense of relief when Ayres decides to return to Australia. But he is also able to leave part of us there, absorbing the beauty and the terror that is Afghanistan and hoping beyond hope that at the very least, the musicians who graduate ANIM will have more positive choices in their futures, just as Eddie Ayres has ultimately been able to forge his required path.' *Loud Mouth—The Music Trust Ezine*

'There are so many memoirs and biographies available these days, very few are written with as much heart as *Danger Music*. Eddie Ayres writes of tremendous hardships, unfathomable in many ways, with humour and most importantly, with understanding. Captivating, moving and relevant . . . this book is one of the best memoirs I've ever read.' The Bibliophile's Bookshelf

Eddie Ayres was born on the White Cliffs of Dover and began playing violin when he was eight years old. He studied viola in Manchester, Berlin and London, played professionally in the UK and Hong Kong and moved to Australia in 2003. Eddie was the presenter of ABC Classic FM's breakfast programme for many years.

Eddie's first book, *Cadence*, is about his journey by bicycle from England to Hong Kong, with only a violin for company.

Eddie was born Emma, and transitioned just before his fiftieth birthday. Better late than never.

Danger
Music

EDDIE AYRES

ALLEN&UNWIN
SYDNEY·MELBOURNE·AUCKLAND·LONDON

This is a true story. Some names and details have been changed to protect privacy.

Allen & Unwin
83 Alexander Street
Crows Nest NSW 2065
Australia
Phone: (61 2) 8425 0100
Email: info@allenandunwin.com
Web: www.allenandunwin.com

A catalogue record for this
book is available from the
National Library of Australia

ISBN 978 1 76052 883 6

Set in Dante MT Pro by Bookhouse, Sydney
Printed and bound in Australia by Griffin Press

10 9 8 7 6 5 4 3 2

The paper in this book is FSC® certified.
FSC® promotes environmentally responsible,
socially beneficial and economically viable
management of the world's forests.

To Dr Sarmast

Contents

These three take crooked ways: carts, boats and musicians.

Prologue

'My name is Fatima, and I want to play the cello.'

'My name is Shahed, and I want to play the viola.'

'My name is Mustaffah, and I want to play the rubab.'

One by one, nearly fifty children stood up and announced which instrument they wanted to learn. They sat tumbled together, two to a chair. There was never a moment of doubt. Every child knew exactly what they wanted to play, which instrument they wanted to dedicate themselves to. This scene might happen in thousands of schools around the world, but in this country it was unique. And it was a miraculous scene, because this was Afghanistan.

Dead end

I was twelve years old when I saw Afghanistan for the first time. It was Christmas Eve 1979 and the Soviet Army had just invaded. On our black-and-white tellie next to the Christmas tree I saw men and a landscape that seemed impossible, living as I did in the temperate realm of Shropshire. The faces of the Afghan people matched their land: the scale of their features, the antiquity of their expression, the uncompromising nature of their world. I wanted to go there; I was desperately unhappy and Afghanistan was as far away as I could imagine.

As I grew older, Afghanistan would appear on the BBC news on a semi-regular basis, pictures of men with magnificent beards and in turbans holding magnificent rocket-propelled grenades, sitting on once-magnificent burnt-out Soviet tanks. The men in *my* world didn't have beards and the most dangerous thing they might hold was a violin. I sometimes thought of the people in Afghanistan and the sounds they might hear, whether you could want to listen to music if you lived in war, or if your mind simply wouldn't make the switch from violence to grace.

The Soviets left in 1989 as I was going to the Hochschule für Musik in West Berlin. The Afghan president, Najibullah, had had some residual support from the Soviets, but with their own collapse the support had dried up. Najibullah tried to please everyone and declared Afghanistan an Islamic state. It didn't work. As I moved to quiet, peaceful Worcester and played Bach with Yehudi Menuhin, Najibullah was overthrown in 1992. He was barred from leaving Kabul and various factional leaders from the mujahideen who had fought the Soviet Army and the Soviet-supported government took over.

The Peshawar peace accord moved to share power with the now fractured elements of the mujahideen; I moved to Hong Kong and joined an orchestra in which we all played together nicely (well, mostly). Afghanistan was always there, just over my shoulder, reminding me how lucky I was to live in an ordered, tranquil world.

My life moved on, and so did Afghanistan's. The country fractured and a civil war ripped the country not into pieces but into shards. Two million people had died in the Afghan–Soviet War. Another four hundred thousand would die by the end of the decade. The Taliban emerged out of the mujahideen and took control of Kabul in 1996. Najibullah, the president from Soviet times, was still holed up in the UN compound after all these years. He believed the Taliban would keep him alive, since they were also Pashtuns, the ethnic group from the east of the country. He was wrong. He was castrated, then dragged behind a truck until he died—and so the Taliban rule of Kabul began.

Up to now, ethnic division had trumped religious division in Afghanistan, hence the endless mess. The Taliban tried to change all that. After the infighting of the mujahideen, the Taliban said that all they wanted was peace; in reality, they violently enforced a way of life that was anathema to the cultured people of Kabul.

In 1997, as I was playing viola in the ceremony to mark the peaceful handover of Hong Kong from the British to the Chinese, Afghans were having to get used to one of the most repressive regimes in history.

The mujahideen had previously banned Kabulis from listening to certain types of music. Now the people of Kabul were banned from listening to or performing music, watching TV, laughing in public, reading anything other than the Koran, taking photographs and putting them up to look at, flying kites and keeping birds (both very popular), shaving their beards off and having Western hairstyles. And if you were female you were banned from education, employment, washing clothes in public, wearing make-up or perfume, going outside without a male relative (and if you did go outside you had to wear a burqa), riding a bike, denying your husband sexual gratification (your husband was allowed to rape you), wearing male clothes, having sex outside of marriage and finally, to end it all, committing suicide.

So, while many people in the world, me included, led our lives in those latter years of the nineties by indulging in music and film and laughter, and doing things we simply would not think twice about like going out on our own, the people of Afghanistan were denied all forms of self-expression. Afghanistan became a B story on the news: every so often, when news time needed to be filled, there would be a story about burqas and internally displaced peoples and women being stoned to death for no apparent reason. Afghanistan became background noise to the world.

I left Hong Kong and made a solo bicycle trip from England back to Hong Kong. As I resettled into regular life and started a radio career, two planes crashed into the World Trade Center and Afghanistan was back on TV screens. Within two months of 9/11, Allied forces had entered Kabul and we were told the Taliban were well and truly defeated.

Afghanistan shadowed me more closely now. As I watched the country emerging from decades of war, I dreamt about cycling there and seeing those stark mountains and ancient faces close up. I didn't. I got caught up in developing a career and being in love, and forgot to check my inner compass. I moved to Australia and worked for the ABC on the radio. Afghanistan moved towards modernity: education for all, girls able to play on the streets, women laughing in public, even reports of a music school being refounded in the west of Kabul by an Afghan–Australian called Dr Sarmast.

I visited the school for the first time in early 2013. The students and staff were all preparing to go on tour to the United States of America, where they would play at Carnegie Hall, the Kennedy Center and the State Department. It was a huge deal. This was the tour that would demonstrate to the US public that all those deaths of soldiers and civilians, all that money spent blowing Afghanistan up then rebuilding it, had been worth it. Here would be an orchestra made up of men and women, playing their own traditional music, but also Western instruments and Western music. It was the epitome of the good news story. In Kabul I was overwhelmed by the passion of the students and the challenges for the staff. After two weeks of teaching and making a radio documentary I was exhausted, but I was also totally hooked. I finally felt I was teaching students to make a real difference in their lives, rather than teaching bored rich kids for whom playing the cello was something to be ticked off on a list of accomplishments.

The US tour was a massive success, not only for the school but also for the US embassy, which had funded it, and the US government. Dr Sarmast and his students were now famous. They had brought Afghan music back from the brink of extinction.

Afghanistan's development seemed to all be going to plan.

And my life was all going to plan.

And then it stopped.

≈

I had a dream job presenting classical music radio. Easy. Don't be late for work, sit in a studio, chat, press the right buttons, go to concerts, chat some more. And that's what I did for nearly a decade. The job of a radio presenter—at least the way I see it—is to be calm, kind, entertaining. A friend to all. Being light and easy is fine if you feel like that, but if you don't feel light and easy, what then?

My life might have seemed shiny and smiley from the outside, but inside my mind was being colonised by depression. It began so subtly. A slight feeling of being off with the world. Tiny frustrations at injustices. Then I slipped to a new level and the smallest annoyance became too much to deal with. I began to lose my concept of joy. Everything seemed to have a smear of putrescence, nothing was healthy, nothing was whole, nothing was simple and happy. I didn't need the Taliban ban on laughing outside; I didn't laugh anywhere.

Depression is leaden and wily. It seeps into every atom and it stops you sleeping, it makes you fat (or thin), it compromises your immune system, it ages every cell, it takes away your self-love, it takes away your sense of humour, it makes you hopeless. I think for me this last was the hardest. All my life, throughout a tough childhood of bullying and a violent home life, I had kept some hope that things would improve. Now, when my life seemed ideal and with no need to be improved, I couldn't see any good, anywhere. I couldn't see any happiness or success.

Depression seems to make you blind, but I also believe it gives you great insight. During this time, as I finally gave up on my ability to work and took sick leave, I started to go to a therapist. Adrienne was perfect. She said it was okay to be depressed. Away from my home life, where I felt guilty about being this way, I could go to Adrienne and speak freely. I could sink back into my depression and try to make friends with it, try to work out what it wanted. We talked about taking antidepressants (I didn't) and how it was okay to use the depression as a way to deeper self-knowledge. But, if there came a time when I simply couldn't do anything, Adrienne would recommend taking the antidepressants.

I felt safe, somehow, in this blanket of melancholy. I knew my melancholy. I was friends with it, finally, which was good as it isolated me from others. Who wants to hang out with a depressed person? I floated outside the world, detached. Eventually it was just melancholy and me, hanging out at home, drinking for two. I listened to ancient choral music. I occasionally rode my bicycle. That was it. I had reached a dead end.

I resigned from the radio. I took sick leave for a month and the ABC managers wrote to me, saying they didn't want me back on air, so that was that. I applied for a job teaching in Scotland and didn't get it. I turned around and around in my life, not seeing any way out, any way in. I felt physically in pain with the claustrophobia of my own brain.

And then, on the news I saw a bomb had gone off during the performance of a play at the French Cultural Centre in Kabul. The man who had refounded the music school in Kabul, Dr Sarmast, had been badly injured and at least five people were killed. Dr Sarmast only survived because he had bent down to pick up his phone at the exact moment the bomb had gone off. It was a suicide bomber, a sixteen-year-old, at a play about suicide bombers. Did the Taliban see the irony? I wrote to Dr Sarmast and said I wanted to apply for the position of cello teacher at the Afghanistan National Institute of Music.

At last I had something to aim for. I practised and practised the cello and sent off my audition tape. I did interviews over Skype, with the foreign staff now dispersed around the world after being temporarily evacuated. I clung to the meagre hope that I might get this job. Moving to a war zone was better than living with what was in my head.

I had to wait.

There is a total purity in sitting in a room on your own, knowing that nobody would miss you for several days, if not weeks, if you died. Over Christmas that year I sank down, crashed through, into new levels of despair. I began to think up ways to top myself. A motorbike crash. Walking into the sea. Pills. Pills and alcohol. And, perhaps the grimmest of all, locking myself in a room and simply not drinking water. I write this now and see how sick I really was.

My friends distilled into the special few. Friends of an older age, who whenever I saw them hugged me and held me in their wisdom for a few hours. And Richard. Sage, calm, in his seventies and still swimming every day in the ocean. I would go over to his house every week and he would lean at the stove carefully making coffee; we would meander through conversations, me never fully admitting how ill I was, he never openly acknowledging that he really knew. These friends were my safety. If they hadn't been there . . . well, they were.

~

In my sessions with Adrienne, the therapist, we had talked about my childhood and my relationship with my mother.

For so many years I had not truly seen what my mother had done for her children, but Adrienne allowed me to love her again. We also talked about moving on from radio, and the importance of making music in my life. I had been so involved in being a radio presenter I had forgotten my roots; I needed to play the cello and the viola again. And finally, after several months, we came to the subject of my own gender identity.

From the age of maybe five, I had always been confounded by having a girl's body. I managed to avoid it influencing me much up to around ten, when tiny breasts began to bud on my chest and Tim, my big brother, told me to put my t-shirt back on. From that instant I was locked into femaleness. At eleven I went to an all-girls school. I started my periods, and grew hips and a contempt for myself that went so deep, in the end, I forgot it was there.

Magical events would happen when people called me a boy. Sometimes this would be embarrassing, for instance when I was about to take off my clothes in a female changing room, but still I would thrill at these little exchanges. I kept my hair short, grew muscles to throw the discus, developed a deep voice and began a very, very long journey of androgyny. At fourteen I realised I was gay. I was at an athletics meeting, waiting for the discus event, and I caught myself staring at a girl hurdler and imagining kissing her. 'Oh fuck. I'm fucking gay.' I look forward to the day when young people will say to themselves, 'Oh great—I'm gay! Woohoo! I can't wait to tell my mum!' Not in England in the early eighties. I managed to hide it for a while, but other girls at school began to sense something was different and kept their distance. I had my first kiss at sixteen. With a girl. Gentle lips. Perfume. Slight fingers on my cheek.

I went to music college at seventeen and felt somehow obliged to try sex with a man. Kissing a woman had been infinitely complex and tantalising; this was harsh, direct, unsubtle. I confirmed for myself that I was a lesbian and confessed to my mum. She ran from the room and didn't talk to me for a day. The grim disappointment in her eyes slowly dissipated as I graduated from college, won a big scholarship and went to West Berlin to study. I then embarked on a serially monogamous love-life. Seven years was consistently the time limit, straight from one deeply loved woman to the next. There was always a point where I couldn't give any more of myself. And then I left. If I'd met myself in a bar, I would have felt sorry for me.

From college to my job in the Hong Kong Philharmonic Orchestra, that was how my twenties spun by. No Taliban limits for me. I drank and partied and ate and travelled myself away from any deeper self-knowledge, until I understood what needed to be done to escape the cycle of semi-pleasure/semi-misery.

I decided I needed to get out and about; in fact, to cycle from the United Kingdom to Hong Kong. I talk about that in another book, *Cadence*, so I won't really go into much detail here, but it was on that trip that I had a profound realisation, one that would take fifteen years to actually do anything about.

I sat in a five-star hotel room in Multan, Pakistan, finally cool after constant fifty-degree days of cycling. I ordered a burger and Coke, and checked what was on the TV. A film, something called *Boys Don't Cry*. Hilary Swank. Sure, seemed good enough for an afternoon away from Pakistan. I pressed play, and soon my life would switch from semi-pleasure/semi-misery to just plain misery.

Boys Don't Cry tells the story of Brandon Teena, a transgender female to male who was raped and murdered by two men in 1993. Brandon had grown up in a trailer park and had tried to join the US Army but failed, because he refused to put down female as his gender. In his short life he never had treatment for gender reassignment, but he presented completely as a man, as the man he knew he was.

I watched this film and I was totally sideswiped. I was so sure of my homosexuality because I had never seen or imagined anything different. Unless a human is extraordinarily individualistic, we tend to mould ourselves roughly around what we see in others. When I was growing up, a woman realising she was really a man simply didn't exist within my view. Very occasionally, I saw males transitioning to females, but they were nearly always the target of spite and ridicule. And there was never any subtlety of differentiation between transgender people, transvestites, homosexuals and drag queens. Quentin Crisp seemed to be enough to depict all of the above. Since society, culture and the media in England were so conservative, I never had the opportunity to see beyond being a lesbian. As far as I knew, there *was* nothing beyond that. I could go down the butch lesbian path, so that's what I did, from when

I was fourteen. To now be presented with this story and this possibility tore me apart. Because I knew it was me.

I fell around in a mist for the next few days. I had to tell someone, but I was alone. In Pakistan. I reached Lahore and decided I would write everything down in a letter to my sister, Liz. She wrote back (poste restante) and said simply that anything I needed to do, she would support me.

When I realised I was transgender, it was a life-destroying moment: I knew from then on that I would never be happy until I did something about it. But to do something about it meant possibly losing everything.

It turned out that I lost everything because I *didn't* do anything about it.

How do people have the bravery to go to a doctor, describe these feelings, have very confronting but beautifully liberating surgery, and take hormones that will completely change their sense of self? Even if everything goes well and works out, still, how does one even begin to do this?

I didn't know, then. I put this knowledge away, very, very tidily, for fifteen years. It sat next to my self-contempt, slowly merging together to build a great depression.

Over the next few years transgender urges would erupt out of me, and I would spend days looking at trans sites on the Internet. Then I would shove everything down again and tell myself it was not necessary to do this thing, that being a butch woman was fine and my girlfriend loves me now, but she had told me very clearly she would leave me if I transitioned, and besides, who would employ you and what would Mum think and everybody will see you as a freak and . . . no. It just wasn't going to happen. I would stay a woman.

∼

There was no work I needed to do while I waited to hear about the Kabul job, so I decided to do what I do best: travel. I looked at my bank balance, and a map. What did I need from this travel? I needed physical activity. I needed beauty. I needed somewhere new. I needed time to meditate, and I needed quiet.

Nepal. I had been looking for a long time at a place called Muktinath, at the top of the Annapurna Circuit. Muktinath is a temple holy to both Hindus and Buddhists. It would be bloody freezing at this time of year, but it was still possible to get there. I could go and see the temple, where dakinis (or sky dancers) were said to inhabit the atmosphere. I could walk alongside my new mate, the black dog, and try to integrate this depression into myself. If I didn't get the job in Kabul, I decided, I would kill myself. That was my plan.

As I walked in Nepal, the devastation of my life became unavoidable. I experienced the honesty of having no idea what would happen to me, all the while waiting to hear if I had got the job in Kabul. I climbed beyond the tree and snow line, wrenched my body into submission, lost ten kilos and practised Vipassana meditation for two hours every day. As the air thinned, my acceptance of my wrecked life thickened. And finally, at the temple in Muktinath, I was blessed by the Hindu priest there and received a state of grace. It was all okay. My relationship had split up, my career, my home, everything had gone. But finally, in a moment, I saw that this was as it needed to be. Something floated away from me in that moment. Horror, profound sadness, a corrupted sense of myself. Rumi tells us in one of his poems to travel inside ourselves if we cannot travel outside. The passages inside are ever-changing, like shafts of light. The light in my head changed from a monotone of dullness to a dappled, kind light.

On the very day I visited the temple in Muktinath, I finally heard that I had got the job in Kabul. This news saved my life. I walked back down the mountain, came back to Australia and slowly felt my depression melt into me. I had faced it, and we had learnt to live with each other. I also realised it would never go away, and I know now that is a good thing, because it allows me to see things for what they really are. What had not killed me had made me stronger.

Springtime sprung for me and a huge energy was released. I rediscovered sex and, on Richard's advice, had a delicious fling with an older woman as I waited for my contract in Kabul to be approved. I swam in the Ladies Baths at Coogee and delighted in the sunshine on my skin, all of me healing in a place where women have swum and bathed for thousands of years. I thought I had come through the worst. I was going to live in a semi-war zone, and finally I felt at peace.

I believed I was fixed.

2

One-way ticket to Kabul

G etting to Afghanistan is surprisingly easy. There is no need to don a helmet, strap yourself into a military plane and sit sideways with a parachute on your back; you don't have to talk nicely to your embassy to get a ride on their next transport. Well, you could try these things, for dramatic effect, or you could just go down to the travel agent and buy a ticket with Emirates to Kabul.

The bigger issue is getting a visa.

I had been to teach at the Afghanistan National Institute of Music (ANIM) three times before I moved there with a job. Each time, I had received an invitation letter from the school and applied for my visa. The first time, the number on the visa didn't match my passport number. I wrote to the embassy in Canberra and asked them about it.

'No problem,' they said. 'Just cross it out with a black pen and write in the correct number.'

I was a little surprised at this DIY approach, and I eventually persuaded them it might be best to send an email to explain that they had made a mistake. It wasn't an issue when I entered the country (well, they did try to tell me), and each time I returned to Kabul I fell more and more in love with the students, the school, the country and its music. And I also began to see just how complex the place was.

A perfect metaphor for Afghanistan is one of their intricate rugs. No matter how long you stare at an Afghan rug you will always see new things, new patterns, new colours and new joys. And these things alter with every change of light. Afghanistan will only ever surprise you, frequently with delight, too often with despair.

This time I was going to live in Kabul for at least two years, so what would I take? My clothes at that time, as any good butch lesbian will attest, were mainly jeans, shorts, men's shirts, t-shirts and leather jackets. These were not going to cut it in Afghanistan. I was going to have to femme it up big-time.

First of all, the head. To appear a little more conventionally female, I let go of my very short haircut and began to grow my hair out. In the Islamic world, women are required to dress modestly and cover their hair and neck, so I bought a few scarves to use as a hijab, or head covering; although I wouldn't need to wear a hijab at the school, I would whenever I was out and about. Which, frankly, wouldn't be that often in a place like Kabul. A hijab shows modesty and hides you from the male gaze. Strictly speaking, as I had already started to get grey hair I didn't need to wear one, but a hijab also helps you to blend in with local people. (As a side note, there is no clear direction in the Koran for women to wear a hijab, only to dress modestly.)

Next, the top half. I needed tops that covered my chest, arms and butt. And, of course, everything else a top usually covers, like your back and stomach. I didn't really want to go down too much of a girly route of puff shoulders and darts, so I was relieved when one day, wandering the streets of Sydney, I found a shop that sold skateboarder and hip-hop clothes. This style, which I thought was pretty damn cool, just happened to surprisingly also score ten out of ten on the Muslim modesty chart, so I bought a bunch of long-sleeved, bottom-covering tops.

As for trousers, they had to be non-revealing of body shape and cover that most inflaming part of women's bodies, the ankle. I look at my substantial ankles now and wonder whether anybody—really, anybody—has ever found my ankles even vaguely alluring. Well, they would never get a chance to in Kabul: those sturdy babies were well covered by my low-crutch hip-hop trousers.

I had sixty kilos of luggage on the flight, as I had also bought a seat for my cello. I slung my new clothes into one suitcase, along with some jeans (I couldn't change my style totally), black concert clothes and the chosen footwear of Australian prime ministers, the diplomatic corps and now roving cello teachers: some R.M. Williams.

I knew I would have to take whatever books I needed with me, so I packed Arnold Schoenberg's *Theory of Harmony* (yes, seriously, he wrote one and it's a great read!), Aaron Copland's *What to Listen for in Music*, Victor Sazer's *New Directions in Cello Playing* (unusual ideas about technique that I was curious to try, more for myself than my students), *Effortless Mastery* by Kenny Werner (my mate Cath, a brilliant cellist, said this book made her even more brilliant), *The Inner Game of Tennis* by W. Timothy Gallwey, a few Buddhist books, including *When Things Fall Apart* by Pema Chodron, and then as many student books as I could fit in: Suzuki cello and viola books, baby duet books, more advanced technical study books and, of course, my own copy of Bach's *Cello Suites*.

My other suitcase was filled with a mobile ultrasound machine. A charity had asked me to take it to Kabul for them, from where it would eventually go to a clinic in Farah, in the far west of the country.

So I was pretty loaded up. J.S. Bach and an ultrasound machine. All the things you need when moving to Afghanistan.

Afghan music can be traced back thousands of years. Because the country lies at the crossroads of many different trading routes, and also because every ethnic group has ties with the same group outside the country, the variety of music in Afghanistan is truly wonderful and ever-changing. There is evidence of ancient Greek music, along with Indian, Persian, Chinese and Arabic music. All these strands weave together into a musical rug, and it is never finished. Perhaps a good way to demonstrate the importance of Afghan music for the rest of the world is to look at the national instrument, the rubab.

The rubab, called the lion of instruments, dates back to at least 700 CE and looks something like a lute. Perhaps the word comes from *ruh*, or soul, and *bab*, doorway. The idea that music opens your soul is a belief in Sufism, and the phrase shows the magic of this instrument. The rubab has three plucked strings; the rest are sympathetic strings, all made from dried, wound sheep gut. The rubab is quite small and is played on the lap of the musician. He or she plays with a pick or *mizrab*, traditionally made from an eagle's talon (a tad hard to come by, so these days the *mizrab* is a bit of plastic). The sound is like the earth itself: since the sympathetic strings give extra vibration, the sound feels like it is coming from deep within the ground. From the rubab is descended the Indian sarod and sarangi, the lute and even the violin, but, unlike the violin, the rubab is made from a single piece of wood taken from the mulberry tree. Mulberry trees grow nearly everywhere in Afghanistan and most gardens in Kabul have at least one—white and red mulberries, good for diabetics and silkworms. Mulberry wood is very hard and would split if you tried to put a nail through it, but fortunately there are no nails in a rubab. Once the wood is hollowed out and shaped, it is covered in goatskin and the fingerboard inlaid with mother-of-pearl. It strikes me writing this that all the essential ingredients of a rubab can be found in any area where there are sheep or goats in Afghanistan. It is truly an instrument of that land.

On one of my previous trips to Kabul I had been invited to visit a master rubab maker at his workshop. Mohammad Esa is the Stradivari of Kabul, but his working conditions didn't exactly demonstrate that: his workshop was half a shipping container on a muddy street in the old part of the city. A panelbeater for aluminium trunks worked in the other half, so the noise was, shall we say, challenging. I had gone with a young bow maker from Australia, Paul Shields, to learn about the different techniques of instrument making. Mohammad sat cross-legged on the floor, a massive slice of tree trunk before him as a workbench. He took an adze (a type of backwards-facing axe dating back to the Stone Age) and hacked away at the inside of a substantial piece of wood. It was extraordinary to see such an ancient way of carving the wood, one that seemed somehow crude but which ended in such delicacy. Mohammad then showed us the mother-of-pearl, which he bought whole from Pakistan, and demonstrated how he carved it into intricate peacocks for the fingerboard, all with the world's biggest file. Here he sat, a great master who had learnt his trade from his father and grandfather. During Taliban times the family had moved to Pakistan, but they kept coming back over the border to get wood, as they believed the quality was better in Afghanistan. They never let go of their skills during the Taliban years; they kept spinning their own vital thread in the musical rug. At one point in our visit Mohammad sat with a rubab in one hand and my viola in the other, a direct line between the two instruments. Without Afghanistan and its history as an ancient trading route and cultural emulsifier, my instrument might never have existed. Without the rubab, the history of musical instruments throughout the whole world might be utterly different. And without Afghan music in general, the history of music in India, the Arab world and Europe would be disparate and possibly unrecognisable.

This was only one of the reasons why music in Afghanistan had to be revived.

~

Those last few days in Sydney, I ate all the food I knew it would be hard to come by in Kabul: fish, salads, dark rye bread, sushi. I drank champagne and toasted my new life with the few friends who had stayed with me through my depression.

There was a small hiccup in my leaving. I had been offered the cello-teaching job in January, but I was still waiting for the contract to be signed by the Afghan minister of education. The minister was responsible for signing the contracts of every single new employee of the ministry, which would certainly keep him or her busy and possibly handicap them from doing something a bit more useful, like developing the education of the country. It was all part of the new push by Afghan President Ashraf Ghani to drive out corruption and nepotism. My contract had not been signed because the minister had not been appointed. Education is a particularly important post, after perhaps the minister of defence and the foreign minister, so it was taking a long time for all the factions within parliament to decide. This, on top of a lengthy holiday for

Nowruz (Shia new year), meant that it had got to the end of March and I still didn't know when I could leave for Kabul.

Finally I wrote to Dr Sarmast and suggested I come as a volunteer for now, and hopefully my contract would be signed before too much time had passed. And so I repacked my bags and rebooked a one-way ticket to Kabul.

Before the civil war, music had been part of every significant event in Afghanistan. There was music for every ethnic group and for every occasion, not only folk music but also classical Afghan music (related to Indian classical music) and Afghan pop. Radio Afghanistan had been fundamentally important in creating a national Afghan identity through its development of a national sound in music, blending different ethnic styles; for many years since the 1940s, the station had encouraged resident musicians to experiment and mix their own styles with others. Mark Slobin, an ethnomusicologist, wrote how Radio Afghanistan's music was 'one of the few manifestations of an emerging pattern of national values and expression'. Music was not being used just as entertainment before it was banned; it had become a vital unifying force for the country.

When the Taliban banned music in 1996, they stole something utterly essential to the Afghan people. I have never before met people who are so soaked in music: to be without music there is to be without life. There is an Afghan proverb that says music is the food for the soul and so, when first the mujahideen then the Taliban banned all music except for

22

religious chanting, the soul of Afghanistan was quickly starved to death.

The Taliban forbade any musician to play their instruments. Anyone who did was severely beaten and their instruments were smashed and burned. Radio Afghanistan, the home of so many musicians, had all its instruments destroyed except for the pianos. Why did they not destroy the pianos? Another instrument that survived was a type of frame drum used by women to accompany their singing. This had been sanctioned by the Prophet Mohammed so was allowed by the Taliban, although women still had to post sentries when they went down to their basements to sing. It is difficult to even imagine all this musical destruction and silence. The horror of Ray Bradbury's *Fahrenheit 451* was lived in reality in Afghanistan during these years in the banning of both books and music.

Unaccompanied chanting, the call to prayer (azan) and recitation of the Koran—all of this was considered outside of music. As in Christian churches during medieval times, and the Orthodox Church still, human voices were acceptable, but any accompaniment by instruments was considered sinful. For some Christians, their belief is very close to fundamental Muslims that musical instruments stir up passions that have no place in worship, or indeed our lives. And that men (and I suppose women as well) should not employ lifeless metals and lifeless wood to praise God.

This ban on music, and the threat of a very severe punishment, did not stop many people from listening to music anyway. Particularly in the western city of Herat, which was heavily anti-Taliban, drivers went around listening to music on their cassette players in their cars. If they were stopped at a checkpoint, they simply ejected the cassette and put in one of Koranic chanting instead. Many musicians emigrated—some to the United States, some to Australia, some to Pakistan—and kept their music alive in relative safety. Some musicians stayed and had to get other jobs to feed their families. One sarangi player had all his instruments destroyed by the Taliban. Then he got a job as a butcher.

I have thought and thought about how this can be equated in Australian society, and wondered whether a sporting comparison might work. Imagine that all forms of sport are completely banned. Every ball, every bat, every racket, every swimming pool, every sporting field around the country is destroyed, and sportspeople are forbidden from ever running or kicking or hitting or throwing or catching or jumping again. And we are all forbidden from talking or writing about sport. Most of our favourite sportspeople move overseas. For the ones who stay, their magnificent bodies gradually atrophy into obesity. We are left to only ever walk at a snail's pace through our lives. Perhaps, now, it might be possible to understand the ban on music in Afghanistan, because music is the very soul of the country.

∿

I arrived at the beginning of April 2015. I had two enormous suitcases (and don't forget the ultrasound machine), two new, smaller cellos for the school, and my own cello and viola. You could say I was burdened.

The approach by air into Kabul is crazily beautiful. The city itself sits in the Kabul River valley, at an altitude of 1600 metres. As the plane takes its obligatory route around the city, you fly over the southern slopes of the Hindu Kush, improbably craggy and close to the wings. The peaks here reach 5000 metres. There is a sense, coming from a world of sea-level living, that this is the land of gods. I had moved beyond a mortal realm. I looked down at the city, in early spring still pale brown but with runs of snow on the mountains and green already in the parks. It seemed appropriate that, in my need to continue on a path of healing and self-knowledge, I had come to live somewhere that felt above the regular world. Afghanistan, in so many ways, was a world apart. I was nearly two kilometres higher in the air than I had been in my depression, and I delighted in the purity of that.

The plane from Dubai was full of rich Afghan men in either traditional dress of payraan tumbaan or snappy Western suits, their wives overly made-up and embracing wriggly children, overweight and highly muscled expat contractors (read: soldiers), and slightly harried charity workers who didn't earn the huge sums that were on offer in some fields. The business section was empty, so no diplomats or drug lords that day. I entertained myself on the plane by trying to guess who did what. The guys with beards and muscles and Arab scarves were easy—something to do with guns—but the older men with briefcases were more of a puzzle. Maybe UN monitoring people, maybe government consultants. There is a saying amongst foreigners in Afghanistan that if you are working in the country you are either a mercenary, a missionary or merely mad. I wasn't going to be earning enough to be a mercenary (even when my contract did arrive). I had come through my madness in the months of depression before and now felt completely sane—that's obviously why I had agreed to a job in one of the most dangerous countries in the world. So, missionary it was. A missionary of music.

The plane landed on a perfect spring afternoon and taxied to the terminal past a library of helicopters and dubious aeroplanes. Every imaginable type was there, some looking like they had been the first ones in during the Soviet invasion. It was an abrupt entry to a very military atmosphere. On landing, nearly all the Afghans stood up straight away, without waiting for the seatbelt sign to go off. I watched the stewards as they shouted at people to sit down; the plane lurched to a near stop mid-taxi and they were forced to sit down by momentum. The pilot clearly had a sense of humour.

I hauled my cello and viola off the plane, and said goodbye to the stewards and the Western world. I had tried to buy some duty-free alcohol on board, but it wasn't being sold. 'We have some little in-flight bottles—we can just give them to you?' said a steward, looking at me with great pity. I declined, not yet knowing how much alcohol was going to become my new best friend.

I wrapped my hijab around my head as best I could and struggled down the stairs to immigration. I have to say now

I hated—*hated*—wearing the hijab. Some women really love it, especially in the winter, but I could never find a comfortable way to wear it that didn't interfere with my peripheral vision. And peripheral vision, especially in Kabul, is a very useful thing.

The Americans (I assume, probably not the Albanians) had equipped the Afghan immigration department with state-of-the-art fingerprint and iris scanners. This was quite a different level of efficiency from the consular official in Canberra, who had suggested I correct the visa number in my passport with black pen. I passed through with my tourist visa. At some point I would need to get a working visa, but that delight lay ahead of me.

The next task on landing was to fill in a foreign registration form. On my other visits there had always been a couple of young men lounging behind a desk and yelling out to the foreigners to give them their photos and fill in the tiny forms. These forms were compulsory, and if you didn't present one on your exit from Kabul you were in serious trouble. Unless you gave a bribe to the official. This time, there was no one at the desk. An interesting decision by whoever was in charge, as this was the main flight of the day for foreigners. I would have to go to the infamous foreign registrations desk in town and get a form there instead.

I chose an older man from the porters touting for work and he guided me through customs. Everything is X-rayed coming into Kabul. Only foreigners are allowed alcohol, and even then only two bottles; anything more is confiscated. But probably not destroyed. I had heard of foreigners emptying out shampoo bottles and filling them with alcohol, just to get a bit more into the country. (I did wonder if it was worth it when you consider what whisky would taste like mixed with a bit of Head & Shoulders. The benefit would be no dandruff on your tonsils.)

As I walked out of the terminal into the delicate sunshine of that spring day, I felt so happy. Simply happy. It had been a long time since I had felt so optimistic about my future. And this was an enormous adventure; I had cycled on my own across continents, learnt the cello in my thirties and presented a national breakfast show for seven years, but this, I knew, was going to be the biggest challenge of my life.

Dr Ahmad Naser Sarmast returned to Kabul in 2008. He was born there and had studied trumpet in the seventies and early eighties at the National School of the Arts, where his father, Salim Sarmast, was director. Salim was the first composer in Afghanistan to write a symphonic score and he conducted a unique orchestra, one made up of Afghan and Western instruments. There are videos of him on the Internet, surrounded by young Afghan musicians—men and women—fervently playing Afghan and Western music. Dr Sarmast left Kabul in the 1980s to study in Russia and, as the Afghan civil war raged and musicians began to be persecuted, he emigrated to Australia with his family in 1994.

As the country was being rebuilt in the early 2000s, Dr Sarmast began negotiating with the Ministry of Education to reinstitute the School of the Arts. Finally, with funding from the World Bank, the US embassy and a number of other donors, the Afghanistan National Institute of Music (ANIM) was inaugurated in 2010. Much of the funding was organised through the Afghanistan Skills Development Project, as part of the Ministry of Education.

Initially Dr Sarmast had wanted the school to be exclusively for street kids and orphans, but the ministry wanted the school to also be available for exceptionally talented children. So an agreement was made: half the places would be reserved for children from poor backgrounds, and the other half would be filled by students who passed an audition. Another exceptional thing about the school was that it would be co-educational, a very, very rare thing in Afghanistan.

At this point in Afghanistan, the female literacy rate was fourteen percent. Not that the male rate was exactly impressive either, at forty-four percent, but to think that only fourteen percent of women in the country could read? That was archaic. The Taliban had banned all girls from attending school and had destroyed any girls' schools they could find, so for ANIM to not only guarantee places for poor kids but to also ensure girls and boys would be educated together was a massive step for the country.

Some people believe that taking steps that are too big can simply end in failure. But there is also a belief, perhaps a more poetic one, that sometimes we have to make a giant leap to achieve any lasting or significant change. For Dr Sarmast, co-education was a giant leap, a gamble not only for the school but also for him personally. He had his father looking over his shoulder as inspiration, but pressure came from all sides: from the Ministry of Education, making sure the curriculum was covering enough academic subjects; from Muslim conservatives, who strongly objected to a music school existing in any way, let alone one that accepted girls; and from the wider music community, who wanted to see the school succeed, but also perhaps felt a sense of jealousy that the school was receiving so much money and so much publicity. All these issues aside, the brutal reality remained that Afghan music had nearly died in the 1990s; this was the best chance yet to tend its meagre flame and let it fully catch fire again.

Pablo Picasso once said, 'The purpose of art is washing the dust of daily life off our souls.' Afghanistan was being rebuilt in many practical ways, but nobody was washing the dust off (and there was a *lot* of dust in Afghanistan). If the country's soul was not being tended to, what was the point of anything?

ANIM was set up as a specialist music school, much like a conservatorium high school. Students entered in grade four and spent one year learning Western music notation, solfège and the recorder, then moved on to learning an instrument in grade five. They graduated in grade twelve, and the highest-achieving students could go on to take an associate degree before completing their studies for a full degree at Kabul University. As well as ANIM's regular academic subjects (English, Dari and Pashto, mathematics, science, history, geography and physical education), there were also Koranic studies and Arabic, and then Hindustani and Western music theory and ear training. Most schools in Kabul ran for a half day, but ANIM began at 8 a.m. and finished at 3 p.m. simply to fit everything in. Aside from being in class, every student was also expected to practise for at least an hour and a half each day, and there was ensemble practice four times a week. Taking instruments home to practise was not really an option since many of the students lived far away, had to squeeze onto crammed buses and often had to hide which school they were attending from their neighbours. A little girl carrying a cello home is the definition of cute in the West, but you might as well paint a target onto the instrument case of a student walking along the street in Kabul. Music might have been being rebuilt in Afghanistan, but not everyone was happy about it.

∼

Kabul Airport is one of the most secure places in the country. There had been an all-out Taliban attack on the airport only recently, and it was a prime target for car bombs and suicide bombs. To get into and out of Kabul, everyone needed to run a gauntlet of foreboding. I saw it as good training. To get into the airport, people with special numberplates could drive straight to the innermost parking area and therefore only go through two security checks; regular folk had to walk a long way from the most distant parking lot and go through six security checks. So, on arrival, only the important people got picked up close to the airport.

The ANIM cars didn't have special numberplates. I had to walk. My ageing porter and I looked in envy at the UN cars and embassy vehicles as we made our way under pine trees to the waiting area for locals. I have always loved watching people at airports, seeing them greet friends and family. Even if I don't know the people themselves, these beautiful human acts often make me cry. Shouts of 'Daddy!' from little girls, mothers rushing forward to greet their children, husbands running to their wives, all this obliterates any doubt about the presence of love in the world. And, of course, in Kabul it was exactly the same, although not quite equal in ebullience. Here were Afghans returning from overseas, and frankly that was something to be celebrated in itself.

I knew that Jennifer, the violin teacher, would be coming to pick me up. I had met her a few months before, a tiny bundle of American energy and optimism, unfettered in her enthusiasm for the country and ANIM. I could see her waving to me from where she stood beside Samir, a student violinist from the school. I had taught Samir many times during my previous visits and had grown very fond of him. He was now seventeen and showed a special musicality and tenderness when he played the violin. I was very touched that he had come to meet me—the arrival of a new foreign teacher was something valued by the students.

I gave Jennifer a hug and shook Samir's hand (since we were in public), then took everything to the ANIM car. The vehicle of choice for most people in Kabul is the Toyota Corolla. If you are rich or extremely worried about your safety, you can drive around in a Toyota Land Cruiser (bulletproofed, this would set you back about US$100,000), but the Corolla was dependable and a decent second-hand one cost around US$10,000. And they blended in perfectly. This would be the security method for my time in Kabul: low profile, blending in, fingers crossed. Foolproof.

$\sim$

Kabul is an ancient city. And over the last forty years it had been through a lot, to put it mildly. Even though it was a sublime day as Wais, the driver, took us through the city to the guesthouse, the ravages of the Soviets, the civil war and, most recently, the Coalition forces were shockingly on display. Kabul was the epitome of a war-torn city trying to get back to normality.

In the sixties the city was elegant, majestic even. Photographs from that time show wide, tree-lined boulevards, a clean river, verdant parks and no barbed wire. Now, fifty years later, the city seemed to contain all the concrete walls in the world. We drove past the embassy and ministry area and could see nothing except cloud-grey walls going up and up into the sky. In places the walls seemed to be twenty metres high, unimaginable even for an Afghan Jack and the Beanstalk. And on the top of the walls, barbed wire. Not just the prickly barbed wire that we might have in Australia to stop sheep, but a particularly cruel barbed wire of razor blades, endlessly curling around the city like a deranged art project. At some points it was clear that people didn't trust the high concrete walls to stop an attack; in a few strategic areas, the high walls were prologued by shorter walls, stout and impassable, a visual preparation for the vertiginously challenged. Some streets had another layer of barrier as well, so the roadway itself became merely a lane; who knows what would have happened if these roads had not started their life so spaciously. There was no sign of an elegant, majestic city anymore.

On corners and next to armoured gates, there were small circular gun posts; it was possible to tell the importance of the building behind the walls according to the weaponry on display at the gun turret. Some merely had a single rifle barrel sticking out, but others had machine guns on the roof manned by surprisingly relaxed-looking soldiers, smoking and grinning.

There was concrete to the sky, but it was also springtime so there were thousands and thousands of rose bushes. As we drove south and west towards the university area, the high walls returned to a friendlier height and the roses multiplied. Pink and white and red and apricot and lavender, lining the roads and reminding us all that beauty will always trump ugliness.

For many foreigners, choosing where to live in Kabul is a moot point. Due to security, nearly every foreigner is obliged by his or her government or company to live in a compound within the secure zone. When I say 'secure zone', that simply means there are higher walls, more guns and more Taliban attacks. So 'secure' is simply a matter of perspective. When I had been to Kabul in the past for shorter visits I had stayed in a foreigners' guesthouse close to the university, but this was now closed after a tragic accident.

A visiting professor had come to stay at the guesthouse and had become a little chilly in the late-winter evening. The oil heating system had already been turned off ahead of the arrival of spring and the air ducts closed, but the professor didn't know that. He turned on his own heater, a bukhari, and died in his sleep from carbon-monoxide poisoning. I learnt a couple of things from this: that in Kabul you were more likely to die from air pollution in your own home than from a bomb, and that I would need somewhere else to stay. Jennifer and Cami, the Colombian percussion teacher and conductor, suggested I live with them at the Italian House, run by a farmer called Giuliano. He, along with two other Italian agriculturalists and Cami and Jennifer lived in a sprawling 1970s house complete with grapevines, peach trees, chickens, sandbags and a pizza oven. Just a few years ago it had been a pizza restaurant—back in Kabul's partying heyday of just after the Coalition invasion, when foreigners could go out in relative safety. The house was just off the main road to the university, behind a scrap-metal dump. It seemed that everywhere was just behind a scrap dump in Kabul.

I had a day to get over jetlag, both time-wise and culturally, and be ready for school. My new life had begun.

3

Lesson one

For a musician, the moment you declare to the world which instrument you want to play is surely one of the most special in your life. It doesn't matter which instrument, it doesn't matter how old you are, it doesn't matter which country you are in—unless you are in Afghanistan, where the event takes on a whole new level of profundity. Because the children who stood up that morning and declared which instrument they wanted to learn were the most precious of musical buds in the world, simply because they lived in such a precarious environment.

Jennifer, Cami and I were to be picked up at 7.30 that morning. I had had seven years of training getting up early for my radio job, and the muezzin in the mosque next door gave the call to prayer at 4.10 a.m. anyway, so I got up at five o'clock, had a coffee and a fag in the garden with the chickens and the flowering peach trees, did an hour of ashtanga yoga (yes, yoga and cigarettes go very well together, thanks for asking) and had a breakfast of flatbread and cheese. I had decided to resurrect my yoga practice after years of neglect. Normally, I would cycle or go for a run, but nobody did that in Kabul. Most people's lives simply didn't need more exercise.

Cami came down to breakfast dapper, beautiful, his green eyes staring back at his wife, Jessica, in Colombia on FaceTime. Cami had come to Afghanistan the previous October to teach music, his reasons the same as any musician: we want to teach music to as many people as possible, especially those with little access to education. Plus, we need to earn money, so we go where the work is. His wife had stayed behind to apply for her US green card and Cami would eventually join her. It was clearly hard for Cami to be apart from Jessica. A hard life, a hard place.

Wais arrived promptly, his massive frame shoved improbably behind the steering wheel. He was to be our regular driver for the short ride to school. Jennifer ran from the house, her hair tucked up neatly in a tight headscarf, hands gripping her breakfast and coffee. Jennifer didn't seem to be an early riser.

We could have walked the distance to school in five minutes, but instead we were stuck in heavy, student-laden traffic along University Road, Afghan music spilling out of Wais' radio. Dr Sarmast had insisted we ride with Wais everywhere, and we were strongly advised against going anywhere other than the school or home. All we were allowed to do was go to the supermarket, and this prospect soon began to attain an equal ranking in excitement to going to the Oscars.

As we drove past Kabul University I saw the new students signing up for the start of the academic year. There were so many of them, all waiting, waiting, waiting, papers in hand, women banding together for protection and social propriety, men pushing from the back of the line. They were all waiting and pushing because they knew it was urgent, important. It was the most important thing in their lives, to get a degree, get a scholarship, get away. It was already heartbreaking.

The school itself lay just beyond the university, in the original buildings for the old School of Fine Arts. Beyond the city I could see the snowy peaks of the Hindu Kush, a constant reminder of magnificence above the drudgery of Kabul. The main ANIM building was a low-slung two-storey block; a new practice-room building stood opposite, beyond a dusty area where the students played cricket and soccer. A wall with barbed wire (natch) surrounded the buildings and the gate had been heavily fortified since my last visit.

Actually, many things had changed in the last few months. There were now armed policemen with Kalashnikovs, whereas before there had only been an extremely surly old man with a frown. The policemen were checking everyone coming in through the armoured gate, students and teachers, so we all had to line up to be searched. This was a cultural lesson in itself: instead of the search being an impersonal affair of peremptory rifling through our bags and a thorough pat down, this was a social occasion. The woman who searched the females sat in a tiny booth, her grandchild perched up on the counter next to a kettle and a fresh naan. She shook my hand, kissed me on both cheeks, asked after my and my family's health and welcomed me to the school. She had eyes like Elizabeth

Taylor, but her life was not one of glamour; she was dressed in drab, shapeless clothing and had a look in her eyes that would become so familiar to me I wouldn't notice it after a while—suffering covered with pride.

School started with an Islamic prayer sung by a tiny student, the kids all lined up in the courtyard amongst the roses and hopeful tufts of grass. Dr Sarmast stood in front like a general, our very own musical warlord, clearly differentiated from the other teachers by his immaculate dress and his optimism. As American helicopters flew low overhead, he presented the new teachers and those who had been given new roles. I was introduced and all the kids I had met before gave me huge smiles and shy little waves. If I had truly expressed my emotions at that moment, I would have wept with joy at the sight of all these young Afghans, over two hundred of them, standing in a place of peace, all waiting to learn. It was a moment of pure hope.

Jennifer told me to stick with her, because things might get a little chaotic.

I have a deeper understanding of that word now.

Assembly ended, and the school year began. Here in the Islamic world, the year was 1394.

We went through the flimsy aluminium doors and I tried to negotiate my way past dozens of children, all taking off their shoes and putting on slippers; although Kabul has a fairly dry climate, somehow there always seemed to be mud everywhere. Jennifer guided me down to the end of the ground-floor corridor, past children shouting out, 'Hello,

Ustad Emma, welcome to Kabul!' She showed me the room that was to be my cello home for the year ahead. It was dark, wood-panelled and looked out onto a maroon wall topped with barbed wire and a tree with leaves so covered in dust I wondered how long it would live.

We and all the students in grade five, most of them around nine or ten years old, went upstairs to the library. There, amongst glass cabinets filled with donated books and sheet music from all around the world, amongst all that kindness, stood Dr Sarmast. He seemed to have an ability to materialise in many places at once.

Now was the great moment of instrument choosing.

One by one the students stood up, said their name, and declared which instrument they wanted to learn.

'My name is Fatima, and I want to learn the cello.'

'My name is Shahed, and I want to learn the viola.'

'My name is Mustaffah, and I want to learn the rubab.'

One by one, a new wave of Afghan musicians. I marvelled that these young people were choosing the viola; kids of this age in Australia probably wouldn't even know what a viola was. According to Jennifer's records, there were enough instruments for everybody to be able to learn what they wanted to, and I now had four little cellists and three little viola players to bring into the musical world.

What a gift. What a responsibility.

Fatima was the first to approach me. She was wary and truly beautiful, with a look of internal ferocity. I sensed there was no mucking around with Fatima. Pedran, handsome and quiet with glasses, looked at me arrogantly, as if I could not possibly meet his expectations. Hashmatullah was the most relaxed-looking of them all, a stout boy with cheeky eyes. He smiled, then stared out of the window at something more interesting. And Meena, pretty, alert, focused, with beads in her hair. I knew immediately she was going to be a star.

We went to find four cellos, and have our first cello lesson.

All the instruments at ANIM were kept upstairs in two barred, padlocked rooms. Like an instrument jail. There were simply hundreds of instruments. Some of them had been bought with funds from the World Bank, but many of them had been donated. All of the Western orchestral instruments were present in abundance, even a Wagner tuba and marching-band drums from a school in the States. These were as yet unused, although the fantasy did flash across my mind of us all, girls and boys, Westerners and Afghans, marching with fanfare through the streets of Kabul, playing Sousa and hitting our marching-band drums as the Taliban looked on approvingly and clapped.

No. That wasn't going to happen.

In the other storeroom were rows and rows of rubabs, tanburs, dilrubas and ghichaks, hanging like a musical meat display. Underneath them were mounds of tablas, all carefully positioned so not one would be damaged. These two rooms probably held most of the instruments in the whole country.

Every single instrument was strictly looked after by Koko (Uncle) Abdul. One might even say savagely looked after. A strict system was in place to make sure no instruments went missing: students had to leave their student card, take their instrument and bring it back at the end of the school day, collecting their card. If not, there were severe consequences. On my previous visits I had seen Koko chase students and teachers down the corridor with a stick, which I later realised was half a violin bow (just how it had been broken was never revealed). Uncle Abdul had been the instrument caretaker at the school for nearly forty years, back when it was the School of Fine Arts; he had left only during the Taliban era, when he moved to Jalalabad. When he had returned, there were no instruments left to look after. Not one. His responsibilities had multiplied somewhat now.

Koko Abdul was a very, very small man, under four foot. Small, perfectly formed, with a David Niven moustache, he had the skin of a ten-year-old and a slightly high-pitched voice, like a viola on its upper string. He was immaculate on this first day of school and every day after, always wearing a perfectly fitted payraan tumbaan, or a child's ski suit when it got cold or he was doing the vacuuming.

I went to the instrument store and tried to be at my most winning. Koko Abdul could be unpredictable, and I didn't want to annoy him on my first day. This man held the keys, literally, to my students' instruments, and therefore to my happiness.

Koko sat behind a small desk covered with various student cards; he was watching a Bollywood film and had his feet next to a heater. As I came in, his moustache twinkled; I bent down and he came and kissed me on the cheek.

The violins and violas were stacked on shelves, but the cellos were standing apart, all in a huddle, as if they didn't trust the other instruments and were keeping to themselves.

There were eight full-size cellos, but my new students were quite a few years off full size themselves. We would be able to use the two new quarter-size cellos I had brought with me, but I needed two more. I found one lurking behind the big ones, and tracked down another in the instrument workshop. All the cellos were good except for this last one. First of all, it had never been varnished, so it sounded like a tin can. Second, at some point it had been damaged on the way to a concert, the neck broken, and, just like a human, if your neck is broken it's hard to go back to quite how you were. It was clear we needed another small cello. And it wouldn't be possible to pop out to a music shop and buy one.

I took the kids down to my room, sent them to find chairs and prepared for their first lesson.

∼

I still remember my own first violin lesson, forty-two years ago now. My teacher, Mrs Llewellyn, taught me how to hold the violin and the bow, but she didn't teach me any music to play for when I went home to my grandma. Unfortunately, this dull first lesson set the tone for the rest (although I did learn some music eventually), and by the time I was twelve I desperately wanted to quit the violin.

My new cello students wouldn't be able to take their instruments home and play something to their grandmas, but I still realised the importance of this first lesson: it was a huge duty to introduce them to the best world of all, the world of music.

And I had to do it in a foreign language.

I had tried to learn a bit of Dari before I moved to Kabul and had picked up a few words on my earlier visits, but this was going to be a whole new challenge. I could feel my brain's synapses sending urgent signals to each other, saying, 'Guys, we have a situation here. New language. New culture. Signs it might be a war zone. A lot of children. Please be advised—this is not a drill. Start new connections now!'

I quickly learnt just how few words you need in order to teach a musical instrument. The first word I learnt was 'relax'. Then 'excellent', 'hand', 'left', 'right', 'shoulder', 'feet', 'one-two-three-four', 'look!', 'listen!', 'heavy', 'light' and 'easy'. I purposely avoided any negative words—I figured these kids had enough negativity in their lives. And so my Dari cello-teaching career began.

~

The first thing any musician should learn is often the last thing we learn: how to bow. (That's bow rhyming with how, not bow rhyming with low.) The art of bowing teaches the student many things: balance, core engagement, co-ordination and timing. But it also teaches grace and self-confidence. Because if you learn bowing at the beginning, the first thing you will have in your new life as a musician is applause.

We all stood in a circle, I breathed in loudly, and we all bowed together, me applauding and cheering. Hashmatullah and Fatima shot each other embarrassed, conspiratorial looks. I got them to copy me as I bowed slowly, then ridiculously fast, straight, a little bit bent, with one foot off the ground, my hands behind my back, cross-eyed, pausing at the bottom. They loved it and Meena smiled the most perfect smile in the world, all dimples and soft ten-year-old cheeks.

The next thing they needed to learn was the same for cellists all around the world: how to sit.

It might seem that the cello is played sitting down. Actually, a cellist is in a position that is almost halfway between sitting and standing. It's an active, engaged sitting. If you are reading this sitting down right now, think about how your body is—are your feet firmly on the floor, ready to lift you at any moment? Do you feel the balance of your body through your feet as you move slightly in the chair? Is your core engaged? Is your back strong in its natural curve and your shoulders relaxed? Is your head in a neutral position? All of this is necessary for the cellist, because you play the cello with your whole body, not just your fingers and arms.

I lined the four neo-cellists up in front of their chairs. We bowed again, and sat down. Hashi plonked himself down in the chair like an exhausted ten-year-old man-boy. He picked at his fingers a bit and scratched his shaven head. Pedran was lighter—alert, aloof. He pushed his glasses up his nose and sneered at me a little.

We all came to the front of our chairs, felt the weight on our two feet, and stood up again. Just like the bowing, I tried to do this as many different ways as I could. We sat down incredibly slowly, then stood up straight away. We sat with our feet off the floor. We sat with our feet together, wide, cross-legged, slumped, but always coming back to the ideal position: legs apart, right foot a little forward, sitting like a mountain with a strong core. The cellists tried this as I walked behind them, trying to push them over. Fatima giggled and Meena concentrated furiously, determined to do everything perfectly. She shot an exasperated look at Fatima, as if to say, 'Fatima, we live in Afghanistan. You live in an orphanage. We are the only four people in the whole country beginning the cello right now. Why are you not listening?'

I had begun to understand on my previous trips how much more patient I had to be with some of the Afghan students. Many of them came from homes where there was an overwhelming amount of stress, and it was a profound, intergenerational stress. Apart from the broader anxieties of the country and city, students also had to deal with living in houses with many other family members, with little privacy or time for reflection. (This was true for every facet of life in Afghanistan, and it was very rare to see an Afghan on their own.) Food was in short supply for some students, along with money and attention from their parents—if they even had a parent. These lessons were possibly one of the rare occasions in these young people's lives when they had truly individual attention from an adult, especially if they came from large families. A student could flash a look of such stress across their face that, if it were Australia, you would be contacting child services.

So when Fatima and Hashi had problems concentrating, I remembered this and we all had a little break. I played them 'Twinkle, Twinkle, Little Star' and they sat dreaming, their small bodies finally in a position they were used to. Learning the cello needs a lot of breaks.

After bowing and sitting, it was time to actually do something with the cellos. Pulling them all carefully out of their cases, I quickly tuned each one with everyone singing along and we stood in front of our chairs. This was the moment when the students would sit down with their instruments for the first time. I had this moment with the cello when I was thirty-three and it was like meeting someone who I knew would be a lifelong friend. It can be an instant of bonding, comfort and great satisfaction.

Or it can be a great big mess.

Meena and Pedran were perfect. They held their left hands around their cellos' necks, made a triangle of their feet and the spike, sat down and tucked the cello perfectly to their hearts. These two were naturals. They wrapped their arms around their cellos and made their first cello hug, faces triumphant.

Hashi had his right hand on the cello, and somehow managed to sit with it ending up on the outside of his legs, like the Queen riding side-saddle. He looked at me with a nervous smile, knowing it wasn't quite right, but not really sure what to do about it.

Some people, young or old, find learning an instrument relatively easy. Setting aside the concept of talent, some people have the ability to copy a complex action with no explanation needed. This is a really fast way to teach, but not every student can do it. Occasionally that action needs to be broken down into smaller and smaller units to allow the student to accomplish it.

So that's what happened with Hashi. By the end of the lesson there were four little cellists, all with the ability to bow, sit, hold their cello, do cello hugs and pluck rhythms on each string. The cello population of Afghanistan had just doubled.

When the other students left, Fatima stayed behind. She looked me directly in the eyes.

'Thank you, teacher.'

Then, embarrassed, she sprinted out of the door.

Four new cello lives had begun and, throughout the whole lesson, an old man in wrinkles and turban peered through the window, beaming toothlessly at us all.

My Afghan life had also begun. The first few days passed in a squall of lessons and sleep, lessons sleep, sleep lessons, and finally it was Friday, our one day off. I was exhausted, as I had never been before. Our days began at 8 a.m. and didn't end before 6 p.m., sometimes long after. I had never worked this hard before in my life. But it didn't matter, because I was exhilarated by my new students, my colleagues, my work, by Kabul itself. Every morning I woke up with the call to prayer and had to remind myself where I was. Kabul was still a city of the TV, of war films and grainy documentaries, not the city where I lived.

∼

Friday was supermarket day. Giuliano shouted up the stairs and asked me if I would like to go to Finest with him, a Western supermarket over in the embassy area. Finest had been attacked by the Taliban in 2011, and eleven people were murdered as they shopped for their biscuits. There were still a few Western supermarkets in Kabul and, if you wanted to kill a few foreigners or rich Afghans, each one was an obvious target.

We drove over in Giuliano's Toyota, like any regular pair going to do their weekly shop. Except that the weekly shop here involved walking past a small militia with automatic weapons, receiving a thorough pat-down, and walking through a maze of heavy steel doors just to get to the cereal section.

Time in Kabul passed in a peculiar way. I had been there less than a week, but it felt like a year. I could hardly remember the smell of the sea, the brush of humidity on my skin, driving in an actual car lane. Every day seemed endless, so walking the aisles of the supermarket, past canned tuna and shortbread and pasta and chocolate and jam, was like going into a distant past. My present had become instant coffee, kebabs and flatbread, and a lot of rice. Here in the supermarket I had so many choices that I found I couldn't decide. Many years ago I met a cellist who had lived in the old Czechoslovakia. He finally moved to the United States, where I had met him. He looked bewildered and told me how he took hours to go shopping, simply because there were so many choices. Something in him seemed to miss Eastern Bloc simplicity.

We finally left with Emmenthal, tagliatelle, Italian coffee, cream and ninety-percent chocolate. A man with a machine gun helped us with our bags.

Friday was a day off, but there was work to do. Dr Sarmast had asked me to rewrite the Western music theory curriculum for the entire school. This meant guiding a student from knowing absolutely nothing about music theory to knowing how to read and write music, and being able to dictate a complex melody, play an intricate rhythmic phrase at sight, and harmonise a Bach chorale. Somehow I felt Friday wasn't going to be quite long enough to work this out. I had a fake beer in the garden and started to read a theory book.

Meena came to her next lesson with dried roses for me from her mother, tied up in a grateful bunch.

Altogether I now had four baby cello students, three older ones, two older double-bass students, three baby viola players and two older ones, called Sonam and Laila.

Jennifer had pointed Laila out to me on that first day. I was busy concentrating on Dr Sarmast speaking when Jennifer told me to look at a young woman who had arrived late. 'That's

Laila, one of your viola students. She's the one Dr Sarmast said is most likely to take over from him.'

A tall girl, seventeen years old, with thick black hair barely covered by a hijab. A broad, dark face with cheekbones so high you could do an Olympic dive off them. She exuded power. And complexity.

Laila was Hazara, the third largest ethnic group in the country. Throughout Afghanistan's history, Hazaras have been brutally discriminated against; it's no surprise that most of the refugees from Afghanistan are Hazara. Nobody knows their origins for sure, but it is likely they are descended from Mongol horsemen. Hazaras are the only ethnic group in Afghanistan without an outside country to support them, as Pakistan did for the Pashtuns, Tajikistan for the Tajiks, and so on. Hazaras are Shia, which means they are the targets of countless Taliban attacks. As I write this, in the comfort of safe, quiet Brisbane, a Shia mosque was just attacked in Kabul by ISIS and around twenty people killed during one of their most important festivals. In July 2016, eighty-four Hazaras were murdered as they demonstrated against the government's electricity development, which excluded the main Hazara area of the country. Hazaras, I'm sure you are getting the message, have been thoroughly shat upon for thousands of years. They have been treated as slaves, had their land stolen from them, been denied basic rights and had development in their districts thwarted. They are dragged off buses and murdered on a regular basis. The school had a large number of Hazaras and many of the other kids shouted 'Jackie Chan' to them. In a friendly way. Mostly.

Fighting has not only been between Hazaras and other ethnic groups—Hazaras also fought each other during the civil war, with smaller and smaller subdivisions fighting and killing. Fighting seemed to never end in Afghanistan. Like an atom always splitting into smaller and smaller parts, fighting, fighting, fighting to eternity. Conflict was in the dust.

I finally met Laila towards the end of the week for her first lesson. As I tuned her viola, in brave, clear English she told me her story.

Laila had taken an unusual path to studying at ANIM. Nearly everyone entered the school in grade four, but Laila had come in grade eight.

As a little girl, Laila loved singing. An aunt suggested she compete in *Afghan Star*, Afghanistan's version of *Australian Idol*. The ninth season was about to start. Laila needed a singing teacher and found out about ANIM. She turned up at the gate and asked to enter. The guard (Naeem, the frowning old man) told her to go away, that there was no place for her, but she begged for help. He showed her where a sitar teacher, Ustad Khan, worked opposite the school. It was the first time Laila had been inside the home of a Tajik, another ethnicity in Afghanistan. She was as nervous as if she were being taken inside a lion's den. In many countries, going into a new teacher's house can be a little intimidating; perhaps they will teach us something we don't understand, or they might not like us. In Afghanistan it is different. Laila was scared to go inside the house because all she knew of Tajiks and Pashtuns was that they killed Hazaras.

Ustad Khan didn't kill her. He asked her to sing. She sang so beautifully the teacher asked her if she wanted to be a musician. She said yes and he took her to ANIM.

When Laila entered ANIM and saw all these instruments for the first time, she felt like she was in a dream. In her words, she 'loved music too much'. She went to Dr Sarmast and asked him if she could attend the school, but he said there was no place for her. She promised him she would work hard, that she would be his best student. He relented and told her to speak with Ustad Shefta, a theory and clarinet teacher, who would help her. Shefta gave her an aural test, which she excelled in. Shefta told her she could become a musician, but she would have to learn in three months what all the other students had learnt over four years. Laila worked hard. She took lessons in flute and theory and, after three months, took an exam. She passed.

Only Laila's mother knew the truth that she was attending music school. At this point, all I learnt was that her father was overseas somewhere, and that Laila lived with her mother and uncle. How do you keep the school you are going to a secret, especially in a place like Kabul, where nobody has any privacy? At first it wasn't a problem, because she and her mother were living alone. But then, once they moved in with the extended family, she had to lie to her uncle and say she was going to another school. Laila would leave home in her regular clothes and change into her uniform at school. How long could this last? And what would happen to Laila if her uncle found out about the school, that she was learning music, that she was studying alongside males? This situation crossed just about every line in traditional Afghan culture.

All this time, hearing her story, I stood with Laila's viola in my hands. It was a beautiful, dark American instrument, a donation from an old viola player. As I handed it to her to start a C-major scale, she said she might not be able to play very well that day. Her uncle had got mad with her and beaten her on the arm. It had hurt so badly, she hadn't been able to play the viola for a week.

The bell rang for the end of the lesson. It was time to teach someone else.

4

If you don't have any problems, get a goat

I sat in my room at the end of the corridor. It was lunchtime, and the students were sitting at tables outside in the dust, eating potatoes, rice and bread. Protein was for another day, another life.

I was overwhelmed. Everything was hard. The only thing that ran smoothly for me in those first few weeks was my sleep. Even that was sometimes disturbed—one night I mistook the panic button for a light switch and woke up the whole neighbourhood with a wild 'The Taliban are attacking!' siren. Someone had taken my nice, cosy Western lifestyle and dumped it in the mirror room at the circus. There were glimpses of what used to be, but then, *boof*. It was gone and only a warped version remained. Nothing was easy, but more difficult than that, nothing was quite what it seemed, nothing worked as you might expect. A simple thing like getting photocopying done could take all day. No paper, the wrong cartridge, then, when all that was fixed, no Internet, no power. It had taken me three weeks just to get a working phone, there was still no sign of my contract, students would show up for lessons then disappear for days at a time. In fact, even days would disappear. The government would suddenly announce a public holiday without any warning, and the whole country would take a break. Apparently it wasn't just cello lessons people needed a break from here—it was life itself.

I began to get grumpy and fractious, deeply frustrated at not being in control of anything. I wasn't even in control of when we went to school or went home; we always had to wait for Wais to finish either taking the students home or bringing Dr Sarmast back from endless meetings at ministries or embassies. I was starting to understand how, after more than a decade of aid, nothing much seemed to have changed in Afghanistan. There was no predictability, but, more importantly, no expectation of predictability.

So I sat in my room, wondering if I could do this job. Tentacles of my old depression writhed around me, seeking an opening. A teenage student came in. I recognised her as the only female trumpet player in the school (and therefore the whole country). People just wandered in and out of rooms at school, even when someone was teaching or practising in them. In Western music schools your practice and teaching space is sacred, but in Kabul I was clearly going to have to give a few firm lessons in knocking on the door. I asked the student how I could help her and she shrugged her shoulders and smiled. I asked the girl her name.

'Bibi Mina,' she replied.

And then she said Mina means love. She smiled and all my frustration just melted away. The only predictability was that I would be endlessly surprised.

∾

Jennifer, Cami and I decided to leave the Italian House and forge our way on our own. We found a house in the district of Kart-e-Char, the Knightsbridge of Kabul. The house was small (therefore easy to heat in the winter) and on a quiet road away from any scrap-metal dump. The street was in the running for the cleanest road in Kabul, with a juice bar round the corner that had been lifted from a B-grade sci-fi movie. This was a Hazara neighbourhood and every day I saw girls walking to school in girl gangs, and women and men strolling the streets eating ice-cream. Kart-e-Char was a little oasis of optimism. The house was owned by a multi-generational Hazara family, who lived next door and immediately proceeded to stare at us from their rooftop through the washing.

Since Jennifer and I teased Cami relentlessly about not really being Colombian but Mexican (it seemed funny at the time), our new place was called the Mexican House.

Our landlord was in his early forties and had just returned from haj, the pilgrimage to Mecca, so, as was his right, we called him haji. Before we moved in, he spent a lot of time planting rose bushes around the large garden and cleaning the house. A couple of American teachers at the Kabul International School had lived there before us, but they had left when the school was closed down because of bomb threats. All foreigners in Kabul were pretty much obliged to have a housekeeper to look after them because of security, and so Shersha came to work for us. Shersha means lion king, and he was. In his early forties, with black curls, slight scoliosis and an endlessly patient look, he took charge of buying everything we needed for the house, and made apple cake for tea.

We moved in just before Jennifer's birthday, at the end of April. Jennifer was clearly a person who knew exactly what she wanted in life, because for her birthday she announced that she wanted a baby goat. Shersha looked at her in discreet disbelief. I had a feeling he had seen this before and knew exactly what getting a goat meant: that he would have to look after it. And that baby goats grow up.

Shersha arrived late in the afternoon on Jennifer's birthday in his 1984 Toyota Corolla taxi; it had a Manchester United badge on the radiator and dollar signs on the doors. He stepped out of the car, lit a cigarette and opened the boot. There, sitting in a mess of wee and poo, was a large goat. It had not been a kid for quite some time.

Since we lived in the Mexican House, everything had to have a Mexican name. The goat was immediately named Nacho, or later, when he was being naughty, Nacho Kebab. He had bits of poo matted in his coat and seemed to have some sort of skin disease; his ribs stuck out through his poo-encrusted coat and he promptly began to eat everything. Even when his ribs didn't stick out anymore, Nacho kept eating. Everything.

It took Nacho just one week to demolish the roses—the flowers, the buds, the leaves and the juicy bits of the stalks—and only then did he start on the grass. Whenever the washing was out on the line, he would eat bits of that too; I would get my laundry back from Shersha with curious designer holes as Nacho would take passing nibbles at hijabs and trousers and shirts. Then, just as we thought things couldn't get any worse, Nacho hit adolescence.

Having continued my healthy habit of having a coffee and a fag in the garden before yoga in the morning, I was now joined by Nacho. Every morning he came and butted me gently on the back and nibbled my ear. I picked bits of poo out of his coat and we really became very good friends, until I realised just how flexible a goat can be. One morning, Nacho seemed to be taking a long time coming to have a tickle with me. I looked over to him and saw only a headless body, with a severe twist to his spine. Thinking he had a tick or something, I went to him just as he was finishing up. Nacho (and this is surely the envy of males everywhere) was blowing himself off. Not only that, he swallowed, bleated and pooed on my foot.

An Afghan proverb: if you don't have any problems, get a goat.

∼

Dr Sarmast danced around the school like Puck, like a samurai, like a god, fixing problems, exhorting staff to work harder, joking, frowning, playing with children, holding them, scolding them. We all loved him, even if some might have resented him for trying to make the school better. To make it better, you had to work harder, and some staff were unenthusiastic about that, to say the least. Lunchtimes should have been sacred, but Dr Sarmast would frequently hold meetings that lasted the whole hour. Who needed food when there was a school to fix, in a land where nothing was stable?

Beyond my job as the cello and double-bass teacher, I was also required to co-teach ear training and Western music theory. Co-teaching actually meant taking the lesson, since the local teachers had some attendance issues. When I found out the local staff only made about $200 a month I understood a little more why they were unmotivated, but it didn't help a tricky situation: I was supposed to help the local teachers follow the curriculum, but, to avoid confrontation, they hadn't actually been told that was my job. I was in a musical minefield.

The theory teacher didn't show up to class. I looked at the curriculum, which I was revising, and stood up in front of the grade tens. They sat at tiny tables, girls in front, with varying scraps of paper as notebooks. A policeman with a Kalashnikov ambled past the window with a teapot and a grin. I could see in the students' faces that they were desperate to learn, to understand a subject that few people in much wealthier countries could understand. Thankfully, Laila was in this class, so she acted as my translator. I asked them a few questions about their most recent lessons and received blank stares. I went back a few more lessons and, still, looks that showed absolutely nothing had been learnt. Back and back I went, until faces began to show some comprehension. So that's where we started. The beginning of the year before.

≈

Allegra came to the rescue.

Allegra was a young American, tall and elegant, with long hair, a sarcastic wit and the blue eyes of a saint. Where Dr Sarmast danced through the school shouting and cajoling, Allegra glided, leaving calm and order in her wake. She was the piano and woodwind teacher and had been at the school for five years. She was also Dr Sarmast's right-hand woman, writing his emails for him, creating proposals for funding and submissions for awards, even filling out visa applications and tending to the pastoral needs of the students. But Allegra was more than even that. Allegra was the foreign teachers' spirit guide, our chaperone through the complexities of Afghan society and politeness. She was married to Shabheer, an Afghan musician, and she had a clear view of how to survive in Afghanistan.

I felt like a foreign invader. I was extremely uncomfortable telling older people, the local teachers, what to do and how to teach, especially as I had just arrived and couldn't even speak the language. I had no experience of teaching Western theory and ear training—why, just because I was a foreigner, would I do any better than them?

Allegra advised me to go ahead and teach the lesson when the other teacher didn't show up, and otherwise just be there for the students. Just being there was more than some teachers could give. I learnt another important lesson from Allegra: in

Afghanistan, if you wait long enough, things will either get fixed or a bigger problem will come along and you'll have to worry about that instead. It was a game of patience, but also one of acceptance. Some might say resignation.

~

Every week we had eight periods of ensemble—orchestra, wind ensemble, Afghan ensemble, qawali group or girls' ensemble.

Afghanistan had had an orchestra before, but there had never been an ensemble only for girls. One day Bibi Mina, the trumpeter who had come into my room not wanting anything but leaving a lot behind, had gone to Dr Sarmast's office. She and her friends were fed up playing with the boys and they wanted their own group. A girls-only space, to be themselves. No boys allowed. Allegra heard about this and decided to start the first ever girls' ensemble in the history of Afghanistan. It began with two violinists, a viola player, two cellists, a trumpeter, one oboist and some percussion. Two years later, when I arrived, there were many, many more players than that. It wasn't just an ensemble. This was a festival, a riot of girl power, Afghan style.

I walked into the ensemble room for my first rehearsal and was struck immediately by the most wonderful problem: there wasn't enough room for everyone. I somehow squeezed myself between the double bass and the tabla, under several violin bows, past the woodwind section and grand piano to behind the cellos. I sat down with Laila and the other older viola player, Sonam.

I had just given a lesson to Sonam. Before she came to ANIM, she had been a street kid, selling chewing gum in traffic jams to help her mum, who was a widow. Now, after five years, Sonam could speak English, read music and played Elgar on the viola. Her life had changed somewhat. She was eighteen, however—a perilous age for poorer girls in Afghanistan, an age when they could be removed from school and given to the best suitor available. One fewer mouth to feed, one fewer future to worry about.

After a half-hour lesson of trying to get Sonam to hold her viola higher (a perennial problem with viola players), she abruptly stopped playing.

'Teacher Emma, I have something to tell you. I am getting married.'

I didn't know how to react. Should I applaud? Should I encourage her to reconsider? What right did I have to make a judgement on this young woman's life? She was getting married to a twenty-five-year-old policeman from Herat—a government job, a safer city, a future beyond anything she could have hoped for five years ago—and it was clear that this was something she wanted to do. I was happy for her. I clapped. As Sonam cleaned her viola to put it away, I said maybe she would have a baby soon to look after.

'No, teacher! First education! Then baby!'

In the ensemble room, I sat down next to Laila and Sonam. The three cellists, Nazira, Shaperai and Hafizah, were mostly strong players so I played viola to help out.

Allegra stood up at the front and the girls chatted on. Nazira played her Bach, Hafizah admired her nails, Sonam looked at her English homework and the percussion players sucked their mallets like lollipops. And still Allegra waited for silence, for the lesson to begin. Marjan, a violinist with green eyes and light brown hair, was the first to notice something was amiss and a wave of attention rippled through the orchestra.

A student called Negin stood up next to Allegra, a baton in hand, her hijab around her neck and her eyes surveying the room. 'Dokhtora,' she cried, meaning 'daughters', or 'girls', '"Laili Jan"!'

And the Afghan Women's Orchestra began to play.

A clarinettist first, a tiny phrase, answered by the oboe. Then the strings, hesitant and awry. As soon as the percussion started, everyone sped off on a joyride of Afghan music, a joyride that could never be equalled, not by Beethoven, not by Bach, not even by Michael Jackson. The girls were playing Afghanistan's own version of *Romeo and Juliet*, 'Laili Jan'.

The lyrics of the song are extremely passionate—a man sings of his lover, Laila, who is breaking his heart. Laila didn't come to visit him at his winter village, but when she finally shows up on the verandah and he asks for a kiss she refuses and his heart is devastated. In every note, every beat of this song, the young girls of the ensemble revealed their true natures. In these moments of making music together, with no man telling them what they should do, what they should wear, how they should behave, they could be totally free. In music there were no 'shoulds'.

When people talk about Afghans, we often think of the firebrand nature of the men and their warlike personalities, the image of a ferocious freedom fighter with a bandolier across his chest and a gleam of revenge in his eyes. That was nothing compared to these girls. They may have had violins in their hands instead of guns, but they were as zealous as any Afghan man. They shot each other vile looks if one player made a mistake, then laughed hysterically with each other over a joke. And when the music came to an end Negin put down her baton and the energy in the room turned once again to gossip, laughter and playing their own music.

I was surprised at how relaxed Allegra was with the girls, how she let them talk and make noise during the rehearsal. I was taught from a very early age to be highly disciplined in rehearsal—no talking, no practising your own part, just concentrating on the collective music. But then I thought about how much these girls had to deal with.

There was Shaperai in the cello section. Shaperai's mother had died giving birth to her and, since she was an only child and her father was a street cleaner, she had been given up to an orphanage to be looked after.

And Cevinch, a tiny thirteen-year-old who loved music so much she had come from Mazar-e-Sharif to study it. It was too dangerous for her to go home by road, too expensive to fly, so she had to stay most of the year away from her family.

And Marjan, the green-eyed girl. Marjan's father had been paralysed in an accident and couldn't work, so her mother worked as a cleaner to support the family. Marjan had a younger sister at the school and a brother, Marshal. Marshal had failed his exams at least two years in a row, but Dr Sarmast couldn't throw him out because if Marshal went, Marjan and her sister would be left without a male escort and they would have to go as well. So Marshal, with a moustache and a teenage anger, was left to study in the grade sixes for eternity.

And the missing girls. The girls who had been at the school, but at the beginning of each term, for varying reasons, didn't return. For marriage, for housework, for propriety. Tahmina was one of these girls. I had met her on my previous trips and I was always impressed by her alertness and quiet, especially amongst the frenzy of ANIM. Tahmina had a younger brother at the school and one day he had returned home and reported to their father that Tahmina had been talking with boys. This clever young woman, around sixteen years old, who was playing Bach and Mozart on the violin, who knew how to play three octave scales, who had played at Carnegie Hall and could harmonise melodies, was now at home. Nothing else. Her brother continued at school and spent his lunchtime talking with girls, girls, girls.

I began to feel an extremely profound level of indignation on behalf of these young women, an indignation that grew, brick by indignant brick. Every time I saw a woman being shouted at by a man, every time I saw a female student being laughed at by a gang of boys, my indignation grew until it became a great anger.

Alongside my indignation was a tiny kernel of dis-ease. Here I was amongst all these young women and I felt entirely 'other'. I tried to put it down to our cultural differences, our ages and our backgrounds, but I knew I was lying to myself. I knew what was re-emerging—the knowledge that I was a woman in body alone.

'Laili Jan' was over. Shaperai took her cello and dragged it like a blanket down the corridor. She laughed at me as I suggested it might be better to pick it up and treat it like a baby.

'Not yet, teacher!' And she pulled her hijab back on her head and made her way out to the world of men.

The school began to settle into its own very particular Afghan rhythm. Western music usually has three or four beats in a bar, but much Afghan music has five or even seven beats in a bar. Five beats for a Western-trained musician is really tricky, but it seems that Afghans are born to an uneven beat. Perhaps it prepares them for things to come. I drove home with Wais one night, five-beat music tumbling from his radio. A man with one leg and a crutch limped down the road; his gait matched the music perfectly.

Laila was making big improvements in her viola playing. Jennifer had been teaching her before I arrived, so she held her instrument and bow beautifully, but we needed to work on her sound. The big difference between the violin and the viola is the tone production. Violinists can use a lighter bow and still get a good sound, but viola players need to sink deep into the viola with the bow to find where the sound lives. This is such good training that Russian violinists often play the viola for a year simply to develop their tone.

I began to understand sound as a metaphor for these young Afghans' voices and positions in the world. To make a good sound, you have to go as far into the instrument as possible. Making a good sound becomes a meditation, a complete commitment to your music, and therefore a statement of who you are. If I could teach Laila anything it was how to make herself heard on the viola, and then perhaps in her country.

To give the bow the best chance to sink into the viola, the viola needs to be horizontal and definitely not droopy. This means that the player needs to stand up straight and not be droopy either. Standing up straight was a problem for Laila. She was a tall, strong young woman, but she slouched; one day we had a lesson only in standing. I measured her height first, then asked her to use her core muscles to lift out of her hips and raise her heart. When I measured her again she had grown three centimetres. Laila told me that after the lesson she would have to go back to slouching. The men in her life didn't want her to stand tall.

Little by little, as her sound opened, Laila revealed more about her life.

When Laila was born, her father was sixty and her mum was about fourteen. Her dad was rich and had bought his wife, although he already had six children from other wives. His new wife only learnt the age of her husband on their wedding day, but he didn't live long after that. Laila's father died in Iran from a heart attack three months before Laila was born. Her mother was left alone, pregnant, at fifteen. Her sons-in-law did not treat her well. They tried to keep her in the house, using her virtually as a slave, but eventually Laila's mum remarried and went with Laila and her new husband to Quetta, in Pakistan. They returned to Afghanistan in 2012.

Back in Kabul, there was a huge fight amongst the extended family over an inheritance, and Laila's family, with two new babies, was thrown out of the house. It was then that Laila was also told that the man she had thought was her father was actually her stepfather. She was devastated—her mother had lied to her. Laila threatened to leave, but her stepfather begged her to stay. Laila went to stay with her paternal brother, but his wife shunned her, not even giving her a pillow at night, calling her an orphan. She started to overeat to the point of vomiting because of stress and anger. After a month she had put on so much weight she hardly knew herself. She was beating herself, and having nightmares every time she slept. She had lived in a place of happiness, but had been born again into a hell.

After six months Laila finally allowed her mum to see her. Laila, like her mother before her, like so many females in Afghanistan, was being worked like a slave by her half-brother. Her mother called her own brother in London, who sent enough money for Laila to go to hospital in India. She eventually returned to Pakistan to live with her aunts and grandmother. In 2014, after much thought, she realised how much she loved her mother and her stepfather, that love was love, that it didn't matter about blood, and she returned to live with them in Kabul.

Laila's stepfather, as so many Hazaras have done before him, decided the best thing for the family was to seek asylum in Australia. He paid a people smuggler and went first to India, then by land to Jakarta. He is still there in a UN camp.

Now Laila's mother was left without a man in her house, and with no money. Her stepson, Laila's half-brother, asked them to return to his family home, promising that everything would be all right. It wasn't. They had gone from only having money problems to now having family and money problems. The stepson's bullying resumed.

Laila had made a practice viola fingerboard from a piece of wood, so that she could do some silent left-hand work at home. Her mother was so terrified that the stepson would find the fingerboard and ask questions that she took it one night and destroyed it.

~

Pedran, the bespectacled baby cellist, had bullied Hashmat into giving him the better cello. Pedran was a little aloof from not only me but also the other students. This was a problem. One afternoon as he was coming out of the instrument store with his cello a boy shoved him to the ground; the cello was cracked in the front and unplayable. Ustad Nader, an ex-army clarinettist who drilled the students in music like a sergeant major in bayoneting, fixed the cello with glue and doggedness. It was never quite the same, so I wrote to some friends in

Australia and asked if they would like to donate some money for a new cello. Little did I know what would come from my small request.

Pedran became a little friendlier to me and laughed at my Dari pronunciation. As I learnt the word for glasses—*oynak*—he pushed his finger through his glasses and poked his eyeball. One lens was totally missing.

Pedran sat with his cello like he was about to play a concerto with the Berlin Philharmonic Orchestra. He was a supremely elegant boy from another age. We played our open string songs, did some rhythm reading, then started work with the bow (*low* this time, not *how*).

The bow is such a strange thing to hold. The aim is to hold it as loosely as possible, but firmly enough that weight can transfer from your hand all the way to the other end of the bow, up to seventy-five centimetres away. It can seem like magic, playing quietly at the end where your hand is, and loudly at the thin end where there doesn't seem to be any weight at all. You can try a bow hold now: hold your right hand out straight like paper for rock, paper, scissors. Then scrunch it up like a rock, but with your fingers over your thumb. And now make a rabbit, your middle fingers forming the teeth over the bent-out thumb or rabbit chin, your outside fingers waving in the air like ears.

Now do exactly the same thing, but put your 'teeth' fingers over a pencil; the ears flop down either side, and your thumb comes up underneath. Soooo simple. And so hard. Jacqueline du Pré said that she had no idea how she held her bow. I'm

71

also reminded of Picasso and his childlike drawings, how we can spend a lifetime trying to return to a child's simplicity. So, if a child can attain that 'simple' bow hold straight away, it is a glorious moment.

And Pedran did. From pencil to thicker pen to bow. Bow exercises like monkey crawls up to the top and windscreen wipers and rocket launchers and writing his name in the air—all the time Pedran kept a hand shape that takes many people years at music college to develop. He had a magnificent talent to copy and experiment and to practise, yet here he was in Kabul being bullied, bullying in turn by fighting Hashi for his cello, and with a single lens for his glasses. I began to feel a great disquiet that Kabul would defeat Pedran's enormous musical capacity before he had really got going.

≈

Shaheer came to live at the Mexican House and worked as our night watchman. This really meant having dinner with us, sleeping in the little house at the end of the garden and occasionally helping out with house stuff.

Shaheer was the twin brother of Shabheer, Allegra's husband. Whereas Shabheer was reasonable, considered and reliable, Shaheer was impetuous, illogical and fickle. He was desperate for work; he had a job at ANIM as a junior staff member, but it only paid $150 a month. He was stuck living with his parents, without any hope of improvement, so at least now he got $50 from the Mexican House and a new place to sleep.

Shaheer was clearly very depressed. He sat every night eating a tiny amount of food very, very slowly, his miniature gymnast's body gradually getting thinner. He played the trombone and trumpet and had performed at Carnegie Hall, but he couldn't see any future for himself in Afghanistan.

'Afghans are okay at everything, experts at nothing. To be an expert you need two luxuries: time and money.'

Shaheer's muscles faded and he talked more and more about leaving, about walking to Germany, about living in a place where he could become an expert at something.

～

It rained for the first time since my arrival. The rain brought down all the pollution in the city, flooded the open sewers and covered everything in brown crap. Jennifer called it 'poop rain', but at least the next morning the air had been scrubbed clean and the Hindu Kush loomed ever closer on the trip to school. A man cycled past with a kitchen sink on his bicycle. I felt, at that moment, I could die and say I'd seen everything.

～

The baby cellists were coming along very nicely. My major challenge in that first term was Hafizah.

Hafizah was one of the older cellists. She was about eighteen at this point and had been at ANIM since the beginning, her photo used regularly for ANIM promotions. What could be more appealing? A young, beautiful Afghan girl playing the most charismatic of Western classical instruments—the cello.

She was a vigorous, determined cellist, but she had learnt the cello on an instrument that was too big for her, so she had some significant technical problems. One of these was refusing to open her legs enough to sit the cello inside her knees as she played. In Afghanistan, a girl opening her legs too much was beyond any decency. I eventually persuaded her, through showing how unstable her cello was, that it really was okay to be just that little un-lady-like and she now grabbed any piece by its notes and played the shit out of it. Hafizah was one of the great characters of the school, a natural leader, magnetic, but prone to gossip. I would often see her whispering with other girls in the corridor, a cruel look on her face.

Her family was very poor. Her father had an illness that sounded like Parkinson's disease, so he couldn't work. Hafizah lived with her parents, sister and brother up one of the steep hillsides, away from electricity or running water. Unlike Western countries, hillsides in Kabul are the domain of the poor. The rich live in the flat areas, or left long ago.

Over the course of just a few days disaster had struck Hafizah's family. First her brother had a motorbike accident and hurt his leg badly. Then her sister was diagnosed with a kidney problem and was taken to hospital. And then her mother fell off the roof of the house and suffered a serious injury to her head. This would be a huge nightmare for any family, but in Afghanistan there is no social net, no government help, no free medical service, no sick leave, no cushion. You fall in Afghanistan, you break. And, if nobody else breaks around you, you are fortunate.

But Hafizah did break. Her father and her mother could not work; she had to look after both of them, and now also her sister and brother. Hafizah was the only vaguely healthy person in the family, but she herself was on a razor's edge of sanity. As the weeks went by, she came to fewer and fewer lessons. At first, not yet being aware of her family life, I wondered if it was because I was giving her technical work to do and maybe she didn't like it.

During lunch one day, Sama, the woman in charge of the office, looked down into the schoolyard below and saw a crowd gathered. She ran down and found Hafizah passed out in the dust. She had simply collapsed from stress.

Hafizah went home that day and came back to school after about a week. When I asked her if she was okay, she nodded and said, 'Yes, teacher, thank you, teacher.' But of course she wasn't. At the end of the lesson she pulled a raw onion on a string up out of the top of her dress; I was half expecting Tony Abbott to appear and gobble it up. Apparently the onion was good for her red eyes, but it couldn't heal her blood-pressure problems; Hafizah fainted again that day. Shit shit shit.

At that moment I wondered about the reason for me being there. I spent my days teaching students to have a straighter bow and play louder. What could music do in the face of such intergenerational suffering?

Jennifer and I gave Hafizah some money for her family. She floated in and out of school over the next few weeks, getting thinner and thinner, more and more determined to stay and study. One day, as I was teaching baby Meena, Hafizah knocked on my door.

'Teacher, I just need quiet.'

And she came and lay down on the floor behind my chair and slept. I covered her with my hijab and kept on teaching.

Negin, the conductor of the girls' ensemble, was becoming more and more confident as a conductor. Standing up in front of a group of musicians and telling them what to do requires a great deal of courage, no matter which country you are in, and Negin had courage spilling out of her hijab. Cami sat quietly beside her and guided her right arm through each bar—down for one, in for two, out for three, up for four. And repeat.

Negin came from a deeply conservative village close to Jalalabad, itself a deeply conservative city close to Pakistan. Negin had been sent to Kabul for school and was living at AFCECO, the orphanage where many of the girls lived. AFCECO called itself an orphanage, but in reality many of the children there had parents who simply could not look after their children. An Italian piano teacher, Adriana, had visited AFCECO back in 2010 and Negin heard the piano for the first time. From this moment she wanted to be a musician and started to attend ANIM. Her mother disapproved, but her father simply said, 'It's your life. Ignore your mother.' Negin had been born into the civil war and Taliban regime, and by this point in her life had never seen or heard any woman playing music.

'I need to play music,' she said to me, defiance flashing in her usually mild eyes.

Negin learnt the rubab first, then switched to the piano. When Allegra started the girls' ensemble there were already two pianists at the keyboard, so Negin became the conductor.

Dr Sarmast had an endless task convincing conservatives in the government and Afghan society that teaching boys and girls together was acceptable. He was also a perpetual hawk, an ever-present eye in the sky, all-seeing, all-knowing. Cami, Jennifer and I started to joke about how he knew everything—our deepest thoughts, our whisky consumption, our illicit trips to bars. Dr Sarmast continually observed the students and their relationships; if a boy and a girl became too close, there was a swift crackdown. This was necessary, and mostly successful. Teenagers, however, are wily, and some relationships flew under even the Sarmast radar.

Negin and a pianist called Elham formed a very close friendship at least a year before I moved to Kabul. Dr Sarmast told them to cool it and it seemed like they had, until somebody found a mobile phone with texts from Elham to Negin. Texts that did not pass Afghan scrutiny. Negin was removed from the school, along with a couple of other girls from her village. Thanks to Dr Sarmast's brilliant diplomacy, Negin was allowed to return to the school after a few months, but the other girls never came back. They joined the missing girls.

Negin and Elham had been warned and had suffered the consequences dearly, but they didn't learn. They continued their closeness, but a few months after Negin's return to the school, Elham won a scholarship to study in the United States. Dr Sarmast told Elham that he had to make a decision: either get engaged to Negin and make it official (this was a good way out as they could disengage later on) or split up with her. Elham chose the latter.

Negin was like a ghost walking through school that day. Normally she would sweep cheer along the corridor with her, but now she was desiccated, a husk at sixteen. Dr Sarmast refused to even look at Elham, who sauntered around the school, cocky and unhindered. It had no effect on him, this ruining of a girl. I began to call him Wickham. There was a rehearsal in my room with Negin, and Dr Sarmast came in to see if she was okay. She sat and he held her as all that extraordinary power of teenage love, the kind that feels like it can never be replaced, came pouring out of her eyes. And I have never seen a kinder, more compassionate look on anyone's face than Dr Sarmast's that day. He would save us all one by one, if only he could.

Negin's father had refused to talk to her when he heard about the whole fiasco. Once again, it took ultimate diplomacy from Dr Sarmast to bring them back together. The day after her tears, Negin walked through the school with her father, proud to introduce him to us, her eyes holding a new look of defiance mixed with pain.

5

Afghan blues

The Mexican House gained three new residents as spring came on: a family of swallows who had returned to their nest in Shaheer's little house. They were named Syri(nx), Lary(nx) and baby Other. I wanted to call them Epi and Glottis but was sadly overruled. Fatty, or La Gordita, Jennifer's cat, spat at them as they flew around, Nacho, her unlikely brother in arms, bleating beside her.

We settled into our new home and accepted its wonderfully eccentric Afghan ways. Unreliable electricity for a start—so unreliable that it surged and failed, burning out plugs and making the light bulbs flash even when they were turned off—and a water system so confusing we never knew if the pump from the well had failed or if the world had run out of water. Shersha, our housekeeper, would smile patiently, press a small black button hidden away and bingo: freshish Kabul water.

Our neighbours, fifteen people in the one extended family, continued to stare at us through the laundry on their rooftop. It was a friendly, curious staring, from the tiny baby all the way up to Bibi, the matriarch. Bibi had been knocked over by a car in a hit-and-run and had a wooden splint on her lower leg. She hobbled round to our house one Friday morning with some of her own naan, keen to see how we foreigners lived. Bibi called Jennifer her daughter and me her son (despite me wearing a hijab to greet her) and insisted we go round to her house for a cup of tea. I was unsure whether to correct Bibi on my gender, but also somehow deeply happy that my innate maleness overcame even the female signifier of a hijab. I decided to let Bibi's beliefs lie undisturbed, as she gave Jennifer and me a tour of their compound. This included proudly showing us a tandoori oven made from a concrete-lined oil drum and a brown sheep standing next to it, looking understandably forlorn; it wouldn't have very far to go for its death at the festival of Eid.

Bibi brought a surprise gift to us the next day: a tiny tortoise, protesting in its shell. We called her Lentita, the Slow One, put her in the grass and never saw her again. A few weeks later Bibi presented us with a larger tortoise—heaven knows where she kept getting them from. The larger one we named Lenti-two and, like a flash, she vanished as well.

Speaking of forlorn, the one lesson I absolutely dreaded every week was teaching ear training to the grade twelves. There were a couple of reasons. One, I am crap at teaching ear training; in Kabul everybody learnt solfège, the method where you sing 'do, re, me' and so on for each note of the scale, but I had never learnt this method. And two, these were some of the trickiest students to teach in the whole school. They were the last few students to have been at the school before Dr Sarmast came, so most of them had extremely poor ear-training skills. I didn't feel I could help them very much, but I did my best.

There were eight of them, all boys, the only survivors of all these years of ANIM. Who knew how many girls should have, could have, been in this class.

Solfège is a system of reading music where you sing a syllable for a note. With its roots in medieval Italy, it reached the height of its popularity with *The Sound of Music* and 'doe, a deer'; from there neither it nor Julie Andrews ever looked back. It is a powerful way of learning music that brings the written music deep into your brain, so that eventually you can sight-read a piece of music just like you are reading this book. For ANIM students who were playing Afghan instruments, and therefore learning everything aurally, it was a big challenge, and of the eight young men in the grade twelves there was only one student who had any chance of passing his exam. This was not good. These eight boys were crucially important to the future success of ANIM. In a few years they could become music teachers in Afghanistan, but if they failed, or if they left, Dr Sarmast would be forever obliged to use foreign staff. If Afghans couldn't do it all themselves eventually, what was the point?

Just as I had done with the theory class, I kept going backwards and backwards, until most of the class understood what I was talking about. And then we practised.

I started with rhythm. We did reading and dictation exercises with the simplest of rhythms, sometimes easier than anything I was doing with the babies. Very few of the students could do even these elementary exercises. Yaqoub, the son of a doctor, glowed with pride when he managed to do what the grade fours were learning: sing a tone and a semitone. This was a bizarre time for me as I wondered what they could have been doing in these lessons for so many years. And then I remembered the local teachers and their attendance patterns. Another important variable in Afghanistan was what the students may have experienced that day, even on the way to school. One morning Mustaffah, a beautiful young chap with thick blue-black curls, seemed more distracted than usual. I asked him what was happening and he said a suicide bomb had exploded on the other side of the bus he was getting off.

Doing endless exercises was necessary, but also frustrating for the students. So I decided to start listening to pieces of music, using them to learn ear-training stuff, a sort of 'hiding the medicine in the chocolate' approach. And it worked. I brought in music by Beethoven, Destiny's Child, Nigel Westlake and some Jewish klezmer music. One day we listened to Cole Porter's 'I Got Rhythm', and Ahmad joined in on tabla. Cole could have asked for more and got it if he had come to Afghanistan.

The students learnt all about thematic development, instrument recognition, song structure and dynamic and tonal variations. All they needed was a story. After we had listened to the atmospheric creaking of Nigel Westlake's 'Wooden Ships', I told them the tale of Shackleton and his miraculous survival in Antarctica. As these young Afghans heard how Shackleton not only saved himself but all his men as well, their faces became intent and completely absorbed in the moment. During that story, and in our listening to 'Wooden Ships', we all forgot about the suicide bombs on the other side of the bus, about the conservative neighbours who disapproved of learning music, about how little hope the students had for the future. They were there, with Shackleton, and he was saving them as well.

The grade twelves might have had rudimentary aural skills, but some of them had mind-blowingly virtuosic instrumental skills. Mustaffah, who had survived the bus bomb, was a beautiful rubab player and Ahmad, the Cole Porter tabla player, was the most thrilling percussionist I think I have ever heard. They loved their music deeply and it shot out of them like bullets from a Kalashnikov. These boys were the freedom fighters for Afghan music.

As the school term went on, I began to notice how quickly the students were aging. One girl in grade eleven, Houma, already had grey hair. She was seventeen. And students who had looked their age only a few weeks ago would, after a weekend, suddenly look middle-aged, with hardened, weary faces. Who knew what had happened over just a few days to make this occur? Perhaps stress, poor diet and water, hard work, no relief. I noticed accelerated aging in myself as well—more grey hair, lines appearing around my forehead. I began to develop a Kabul Eleven: two vertical lines on my forehead that grew deeper and deeper as I found out more and more of the tragedy of Afghanistan.

~

Amruddin was the senior bass player in the school. He was about nineteen, with an obsessively maintained rockabilly hairstyle, sometimes dyed brown, sometimes a hint of purple. Amruddin was a dude. He had been playing the bass for about four years and made an opulent sound. I practised the double bass for about an hour after school every day to catch up with him, and we learnt side by side. It didn't take long to discover that Amruddin had, again, very poor knowledge of the most fundamental Western music building blocks, such as scales and simple rhythms. He was extremely good-natured about this and diligently practised everything I gave him. He took videos of me playing on his phone until it was stolen and he couldn't afford to buy another one.

I played him a variety of music—some Joni Mitchell, some Jason Isbell, some Jacques Loussier—and he loved it all. We also listened to blues, as he was playing a blues bass line.

'Teacher, what is this blue? Why not red or white?'

After explaining how blues came from African–American slaves and how it should be played at the same speed that a defeated man would shuffle at, Amruddin said, 'Teacher, this is Afghanistan.'

~

Hafizah continued to drift in and out of school. I was never sure when she would come for a lesson, but if she wasn't there I always had a baby to teach instead. Or Shaperai.

Iftar at the Mexican house. From left to right: Shabheer, Cami, Allegra, Jennifer, and Shaheer stroking Fatty. Who knows what Nacho is up to at the back.

Two new besties. A rest on a motorbike ride up TV Hill, in the middle of Kabul.

I like to think of this as my 'Bride of ISIS' portrait. Then again, I'd rather not.

Hanging at home on a Friday. Finally, with my new chest, I can try to rock a James Dean look. It's a work in progress. *(Photographer: Andrew Quilty)*

On my bike on the way to a boxing match. Andrew Quilty spent the whole day sitting backwards on Alex's bike to take photos of me for *Good Weekend* magazine. That man is a genius with very, very good balance. *(Photographer: Andrew Quilty)*

Allegra in down-face dog pose. Eidie, our yoga master, is taking a paws-on approach to coaching.

Pancha. Pancha was perfect.

Wais's gun at lunch.
Delicious with a fresh
tomato salad.

35|00

teacher Allegra, EMa, Jennifer they very very, very good teacher. whrite of Aziza

Aziza's gift on my whiteboard one morning.

Cami, Nacho and Jennifer before the British Charity Ball. Nacho declined his invitation to go, despite clearly wearing the correct colours.

The remains of the Darul Aman Palace; built in the 1920s by King Amanullah Khan as a drive to modernise Afghanistan, destroyed in the Civil War, and now being restored with money from the United States, fingers crossed.

Bamiyan. The view from inside one of the great holes left by the destroyed Buddha statues. Such beauty, such terror.

Dragon Valley, Bamiyan, and a shrine to Ali, the son-in-law of the Prophet Mohammed. Just over the hill lies a grim village for returning Hazara refugees from Iran and Pakistan.

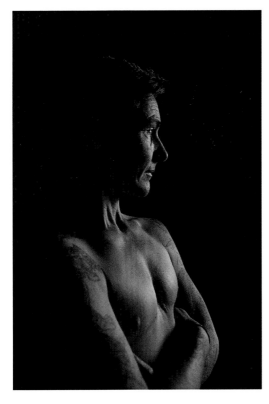

I am so grateful to Andrew for this photo. It shows all the strain, sadness and strength in my life at that time. *(Photographer: Andrew Quilty)*

My big sister Liz on her birthday in Cheshire. Liz has been my guardian angel my whole life. So I gave her a cake.

Carol and me, Loch Ness, July 2016. Ease, Joy and Glory. And no monsters.

She of cello-dragging fame, Shaperai had a long, elegant nose and huge eyes, straight from a Persian miniature painting. She was sharp and witty and was adored by the other students. She would say something very fast in Dari so I had no chance of understanding it, and the other girls would fall around laughing. When Shaperai played her cello, a mournful expression would descend over her face and she became a poet. Shaperai was an extraordinarily dedicated student and demanded a lesson whenever I was alone. This usually took the line of 'Teacher!' and a foot stamp. I pointed out to her that I had a few other things to do, like lesson planning and curriculum revising, but she would never, ever take no for an answer. I loved this about Shaperai, and, although her technique remained awkward and her rhythm chaotic, for pure effort she was my star pupil.

Hafizah slowly brightened up. I knew this was happening because she started to paint her nails again and took more care with her appearance. Hafizah had a unique dress sense and would always match her shoes with her hijab and top and, of course, her nail varnish. The students came to school in their own clothes for the first few weeks, then a tide of maroon and grey cloth haphazardly washed through them, as their uniforms were finished by a tailor. Hafizah was not at all thwarted when her uniform was ready to be worn; on top of the drab long grey dress and trousers there was always a little touch of jewellery, nail polish and make-up. Hafizah delighted in this world and gave me fashion advice, which would normally involve suggesting I wear more feminine clothes. She would often stay in my room with another girl, painting their nails together and muttering indistinctly to each other. When Hafizah recovered, the whole school felt better. She was the mother student.

One day I had been delayed getting to orchestra for some reason and rushed in late to rehearsal. Jennifer was conducting the orchestra and, just as I came in, she asked Hafizah if she was okay. Hafizah looked terrible. She had turned a yellowish white and her little body was slumped behind her cello. With a jolt, she ran from the room. I raced after her and found her outside, gasping for breath. She was clearly having a panic attack. I made sure her hijab was loose and tried to get her to slow her breathing down. After a few minutes this seemed to work, but then she crumpled into a sea of weeping. Heaving sobs, her whole gaunt body. I held her shoulders and just sat with her there, under the trees, next to the peach and pink roses. It was heartbreaking. She eventually said that when people talk a lot, and loudly (Jennifer in orchestra), she couldn't breathe and needed to be in silence. So I stayed quietly with her until she stopped, then walked with her upstairs for Parwana and Sama to take care of her. This single human tragedy.

For days after that, Hafizah would return to my room to rest. She lay there as I taught the babies their Twinkles. I think she was comforted by that. Comforted by them, that they hadn't learnt to be disappointed yet.

~

The girls faced the stresses of having to do their schoolwork on top of relentless housework, but the boys had their stresses too. Samir, a grade eleven violinist, had had to take on financial responsibility for his family because his father couldn't get any work. Samir played Afghan music brilliantly and he was often hired for weddings. These would normally go far into the night, so Samir would turn up the next day at school useless for any learning. In many ways, the school had totally done its job by giving this man a livelihood and enabling Afghan music to continue through his hands.

When it came to Western music, though, Samir was totally lost and could hardly play a scale or read a rhythm accurately. Why were these students not concentrating on Afghan music, when for the vast majority of them it was the music they loved? It seemed obvious that a student like Samir would never play Mozart or Vivaldi again once he left ANIM, so why make him play it when it took him away from what he excelled at?

Another boy who clearly felt the stress of having to provide for his family was Marshal. Marshal, brother of the green-eyed violinist Marjan, and a grown boy-man still in grade six, was the only male in the family capable of work. Unfortunately, he saw theft as a viable means to make money.

Diana, a new piano teacher, had arrived from Russia. After a few weeks she said that she had lost her passport and her wallet, which had quite a lot of money in it. Dr Sarmast investigated and Marshal, who had just taken a class with Diana that day, admitted to the theft. He had taken the passport and tried to sell it, with no luck. This was crunch time for Marshal. He had failed his exams at least two years in a row, he had been caught stealing before, and the only reason he was still at school was to be a male escort for his two much more intelligent and hard-working sisters. Dr Sarmast did the only thing he should—he expelled Marshal. For a week Marjan and her sister failed to come to school. One morning I saw their mother coming down the stairs from Dr Sarmast's office. She was a magnificent woman, a headmistress or a duchess in another life. She descended the stairs with the heaviness of life in her shoulders and an ashamed, beseeching look in her face. It turned out that both the girls had stipends from the school and this money was so vital for the whole family that the two sisters came back the next day. In a rare gender flip, their brother stayed at home.

Laila stood in my room listening to a recording of Hindemith's Viola Sonata Op. 25. Hindemith's direction in the fourth movement is that tone quality is of secondary importance. The movement is a string of rapid notes, all the same length, with no metre or dynamic other than VERY LOUD.

'But, Teacher Emma, this music is so hard to listen to, never mind play.'

I had been talking with Laila about mind practice. Since her mother had burnt her practice fingerboard, Laila, like most of the other students, had no way to practise outside school. I told her about learning the Hindemith when I was at college, and how I did most of the practice in my mind. So when she went home at night and did all the housework for the males in the family, she could at least have her music with her, running through her brain.

Laila was highly stressed, not only about her home life but also about the country at large. She was utterly passionate about Afghanistan and, while she wanted to go overseas to study, she was determined to return to her country and help rebuild it. Laila was deeply affected by political events in Afghanistan, particularly whenever yet another tale of corruption came up. We had been talking about a school cook from a while back who had stolen meat from the ANIM children to take home for his own.

'The problem with this country is that everybody does things for themselves only.'

I became more and more worried about Laila. I found out that not only did she have all the pressures of schoolwork and housework, but she also had a job cleaning dishes after school at a restaurant. She seemed to only get about four hours' sleep a day. Her face began to show it—the skin under her eyes darkened and her eyes lost their gleam.

Jennifer and I went to Dr Sarmast to see if he could do anything to help. If something was getting in the way of a girl succeeding at school, Dr Sarmast was the man to sort it out.

And he did. Jennifer's sister in the States had been waiting for a student to help, so she began to sponsor Laila with a monthly stipend. This meant that Laila could at least stop washing dishes. Her uncles and brothers would never allow her to stop anything else.

'But, Teacher Emma, Teacher Jennifer, is it right? Should I take this money?'

'It's totally okay, Laila,' I replied. 'And, when you are older, you will sponsor someone yourself.'

'Of course I will.'

~

The National Youth Orchestra of Afghanistan rehearsed twice a week at school. The orchestra had both Western and Afghan instruments, and Allegra and Cami made arrangements of Western and Afghan music especially for this group of players. The combination of instruments made a sound so unique that it brought tears to my eyes on a regular basis. The orchestra had about forty players in it, from grade six violinists to grade fourteen percussionists. Girls and boys. Hazara, Tajik, Pashtun, Uzbek. This was the dream of Dr Sarmast brought to life. A resounding life.

Orchestra time started with a battle to find a music stand. This is an international, age-old tradition, like musical chairs but with, um, musical stands. No matter where I have taught and played, there always seems to be one too few music stands for the players; on top of this, the students at ANIM were quite ruthless about taking your stand if you didn't guard it. The next battle was fitting everyone into the not-so-big rehearsal room. Unfortunately, the percussion players were often the last to arrive; once the strings, brass, woodwind and Afghan instruments were in, suddenly Masjedi or Qambar would show up at the door with two timpani, a marimba and a grin, expecting to come in. I suggested they show up a little earlier, and they flashed their perfect smiles at me, held their hands on their hearts, and promised they would.

One of the junior staff, a skinny young man in mullet and glasses called Milad, conducted the orchestra. There were five junior staff, all graduates from the previous year: Shaheer, trumpet, Masjedi, percussion, Sameem, tabla, Fayez, violin and Milad, piano and conducting. These men were the most important part of the school in many ways, as they were its past, present and future. Dr Sarmast's plan was to have a totally Afghan staff after a few years and for the school to be completely sustainable. When each year graduated, the best students would be invited to become teachers, and so the staff would be built up and up. Foreign teachers would become a distant memory.

Milad had started playing the piano with Adriana, the Italian teacher who had introduced piano to Negin. He was an exquisite pianist, drawing melancholy and melody from every piece he played. On a previous visit I had been walking with Milad from a concert at the German embassy and he had pointed at the full moon.

'I am going to play that sonata one day.'

Milad was applying for scholarships in the US and had been accepted to a couple of places, but he still needed to pass his English TOEFL exam. I spoke as often as I could with him to help with his grammar, as I knew how hard those exams were.

As in the girls' ensemble, I played the viola in orchestra. I positioned myself between Sonam and Laila, three to a stand in true school fashion. (This would never happen in a professional orchestra—sitting three to a stand is terrible for your posture, never mind your older eyesight.) Milad announced the piece we would play that day—Mozart's 'Turkish March'.

The Afghan instrumentalists sat at the feet of the conductor, with the Western instrumentalists on chairs around them. The rubab players started with the main tune, faster than Milad was conducting, but totally thrilling. I imagined Mozart on his viola beside Laila and Sonam, and wondered what he would have thought about this orchestra playing his music, how much he would have loved the vibrancy of their sound. The piece is a simple tune, but with all these new layers of Afghan and Western tones it glistened.

The viola part was very simple and mainly involved the ability to count rests accurately. Sonam sat uninterested, her viola drooping and her fingers dropping on the fingerboard almost randomly. Although Laila had been playing for much less time than Sonam, her attitude was completely different. She sat alert and involved, as if she had the main tune all the time, instead of the offbeats. At one point Laila turned to me and asked, 'Teacher Emma, why do bad habits come easier?'

The students played with each other not perhaps in the way that students in the West would, as brothers and sisters in art, but rather as brothers and sisters in arms. There was something territorial and brutal about their playing. This sounds negative, but it wasn't. It was completely captivating. The students, once they were sure of their parts, played with wild confidence. In the West, young musicians play with a softness that invites another musician in. In Kabul, it was as if they were daring each other to come along for the ride.

∽

One of the big issues with having Western instruments at ANIM was that a Westerner was generally needed to teach them. There had been a trumpeter from the States when ANIM started, but he had left abruptly, along with the cello teacher. Another American teacher came but, sadly, he appeared to have some mental-health issues and left in the middle of the night as well. So there had not been a trumpet teacher at ANIM for close to two years. This did nothing to deter the trumpeters. The oldest was a chap called Tamim, but the best was Baset, a nerdy-looking sixteen-year-old with thick glasses, an American military hairstyle and a determination unequalled by any.

The thing that distinguished Baset from most of the other students and junior staff was his ability to dream, and then act on his dreams.

These young Afghans were growing up in the Facebook generation. Through their phones they could see the outside world; it was presented to them every day, in all its falseness and exaggeration. The students believed everything they read on Facebook, and they could see the possibilities and security outside of Afghanistan like no one had done since the seventies. Some students started to talk about running, about going overseas and not coming back. There were opportunities for this—two students had stayed in Denmark after a teacher-training course, a rock band had stayed in Switzerland after a festival, and one student had stayed in London after a concert. Nobody had escaped on the US tour because there was security with them every day to stop exactly that from happening. Baset saw all this and used the unstoppable energy of his desires to chase his dreams.

Baset billed himself on Facebook, quite accurately, as the best trumpeter in Afghanistan. He had not had regular lessons for a long time, yet he stayed behind after school every day practising his scales, exercises, even the Haydn Trumpet Concerto. When Baset was around, the school sounded like any music school in the world. Baset was trying to get to the States to study at Interlochen, a leading music high school—and, if anyone could get themselves from Kabul to the States with virtually no teaching, Baset was the one.

Jennifer was the Mexican House social secretary. She had the most remarkable ability to make friends and, very important in Kabul, get invitations to places that had alcohol. Time and alcohol had quickly become my most valued assets here. One night Jennifer announced that we were all on the list to go to the EU Delegation bar, which was within the EU compound.

Getting on the list for an event there was crucial. No name; no entry. With a gun stuck in your face. It was like an uber LA-style thing, where getting on the list was the difference between being cool or not, getting a Guinness or not. To get into an embassy, however, you had to slowly unpeel the onion of security. The first layer was Afghan police, who simply wouldn't let you into the area if your name wasn't on the list. Then a layer of usually Nepalese guards, who wouldn't let you in if your name wasn't on the list (even though your name had to be on the list for you to have come that far). And then the inner layer: security contractors from the country of the embassy you were visiting, who wouldn't let you in if your name wasn't on the list. As these layers peeled away, the guns and uniforms and attitude and biceps improved dramatically. From the often messy attire of Afghan soldiers with their ancient Kalashnikovs to the scrupulously disciplined appearance of the embassy staff with automatic weapons like pieces of art under their arms. But all of them ready, their guns in shooting position, tucked under their armpit like a violinist ready to play a concert.

Jennifer, Cami and I took a taxi in the early evening to the outer layer. There were a few taxi companies in Kabul that were safe for foreigners—which is to say the drivers got paid enough that they weren't tempted to sell you to a kidnapping gang. We drove past the amusement park with its big dipper, past the night-time kebab sellers, past the blue stones on the pavement that were women in burqas begging. All this time, Jennifer, with a perfect Broadway voice, sang Afghanistan's unofficial national anthem, 'My Heart Will Go On'. Somehow, *Titanic* had made it past the Taliban in the nineties and never sunk.

We arrived at the police checkpoint outside the EU complex. Our name was on the list, so we made our way through the first layer. We walked down a tree-lined street and I suddenly realised that everything felt, well, normal. We were walking. It was raining. We were going out for a drink. We had just been dropped off in a taxi. Sure, there were men around with guns staring at us, but otherwise it was just a regular Thursday night. In Kabul.

We finally made it through to the compound itself. For weeks up to this point I had only been to school then back home again; although both those places had their charms, I had forgotten just how charming a place could be. We walked into the compound garden and I felt like Lucy from *The Lion, the Witch and the Wardrobe* when she enters Narnia for the first time. There was what seemed like acres of grass. Not tufty grass, but smooth, Wimbledon grass. There was a swimming pool. There were buildings that were finished and smooth and clean. And there was no barbed wire. Well, there had to be barbed wire somewhere, but this place was so big that the barbed wire for once was out of sight. And out of sight, out of mind. I ordered a Guinness.

The EU compound seemed like a place outside of Kabul—in fact, it seemed like a small town in Switzerland—but of course the conversation was completely about Kabul. I talked with an American psychiatrist who told me about his work in the country.

You might think that for a war-torn country, with nearly everyone being affected by violence in some way or another, there would be plenty of psychiatric or psychological services. Everyone in Afghanistan suffered from post-traumatic stress disorder in some form. With all the billions spent in Afghanistan, wouldn't it be possible to help people to not remain completely fucked in the head?

There have been around one hundred billion US dollars given by the United States alone to Afghanistan. Let's have a look at that number. First of all, it's unimaginable: 100,000,000,000. A million, multiplied by a thousand, multiplied by one hundred. If you put it into Google, you get a picture of Dr Evil from *Austin Powers*.

When I was writing this I considered typing out a billion a hundred times, but then I thought, nah.

Oh bugger it, I'm going to.

billion billion

I counted it, but go ahead and double check. Please read each one out loud and remember, each of those billions is a thousand million. Another way to think about how fucking huge this number is that it would take one person five thousand years just to count every single dollar.

There are many, many articles from very reputable sources about how aid has been mismanaged in Afghanistan, so I can't really add anything here. But when I found out from the psychiatrist that in the whole of Afghanistan there is only one psychiatric hospital, and in that hospital there are only one hundred beds, a little bit of me withered. I looked around me that night: I saw the lawns, I saw the armour-plated four-wheel drives, I saw the expats who were not allowed to leave the compound without bulletproof jackets inside a bulletproof car with armed guards, I saw the buildings with their European fittings, I saw the swimming pool, and I felt that something was very, very wrong.

Mohammad was a true musician. He played the guitar. Actually, he didn't just play the guitar, he loved the guitar, worshipping and caressing it with his fine-boned, hairy fingers. Mohammad was always practising and worked much harder than the actual guitar teacher at helping the young players at ANIM. Mohammad was also Hashmatullah's older brother and came to me every week to check on his progress. Mohammad was extraordinarily entrepreneurial and had set up a tourist business in Kabul; I'm not sure what this involved, but there was a small amount of internal tourism in Afghanistan. He had spent US$10,000 on an office and was making his way in the world.

Mohammad was on the up.

Allegra introduced me to Mohammad. He had the type of Afghan charm and courtesy that is unequalled anywhere in the world, apart from Pakistan. It was an ability to make you the centre of his world, and for you to believe he would do absolutely anything to make you happy and comfortable in his country. Mohammad truly appreciated the foreign teachers and came often to my room to play me pieces he had composed for the guitar. He was a small, skinny man, already balding. All the hair that would have been on his head had clearly decided it was more fun to live on his chest; there was quite the hirsute celebration going on beneath his shirt.

Mohammad would have been about twenty-three when I knew him, so had been just a small child in the Taliban era. Somehow, even though the Taliban had banned music, Mohammad had got hold of a cassette player and found music for himself. He must have known how dangerous it was to listen to music because he took his cassette player to a storm drain in Kabul and there, amongst the rubbish and the shit and the cold, listened to music. That is why he was a true musician.

It's perhaps hard to imagine in Australia how feared the Taliban were. Shabheer, Allegra's husband, said that the Taliban were so powerful, all they had to do was leave a turban on a chair in the middle of the street for you to know that they were there, they were watching, they were listening. The Taliban heard Mohammad's music, dragged the tiny kid out of the drain and took him home. They had no remorse in beating this six-year-old boy. They beat his father as well, just in case Mohammad forgot.

He didn't forget. But he did go back to the storm drain, found his cassette player and carried on listening to his music. The Taliban didn't bother beating him up this time. They put his father in jail for a year instead.

～

Imprisoned in my hijab, I became fascinated with the men in Afghanistan. On the street, at police blockades, in shops, at school, men everywhere treated each other with a tenderness and love that would never be demonstrated in Australia. Men held hands as they walked along the street, they sat close to each other in class, they whispered in each other's ears. Men provided an intimacy for each other that straight men would only demonstrate with women in Australia. It seemed that the only time an Afghan man was truly himself was when he was with another man. As men greeted each other, they pulled each other in close and gave the most delicate of kisses on each cheek. As a foreign woman, I was occasionally treated to this and it astounded me every time. The gossamer subtlety of their touch.

Wais, the driver, and Shersha, our lion king, were the most entertaining pair to watch. Wais was an enormous man, close to two metres tall and at least one hundred and fifty kilos. Shersha was slight and small, compact. Wais drove us home and greeted Shersha with a bear hug, then wrestled with him around the yard like two puppies.

Wais should really have had his own TV show in Afghanistan. Every morning he came early to the Mexican House and we gave him coffee and a fag. He sat on a tiny chair, his huge bulk threatening the chair's abilities, smoothing his comb-over and teasing us about everything. He made prank calls to Wali at the front gate. He chased Nacho. He mocked Beethoven's music as boring. If Jennifer was still upstairs, Wais would ask if she was dead. His favourite phrase was '*Boombori!*' ('Go and die!'). When I got my first *Boombori!* from Wais, I knew he liked me.

Riding to school with him was like being in the back of a Toyota Corolla driven by Sterling Moss on speed, with a few Afghan police and some traffic thrown in for entertainment. Nobody seemed to care how fast you drove in Kabul, so when the roads were free, and sometimes even when they weren't, Wais drove at eighty or even one hundred kilometres an hour, weaving, dodging, skidding down the road to school.

'Faster, Wais, faster!' I told him, addicted to nearly dying, twice a day. Riding to school with Wais was a drug, and I loved that man. We all did.

∼

It started very slowly. I had been teaching grade eleven ear training and one day a student, Rameen, wasn't there. I marked him absent. The next week he wasn't there either. I asked his friend where he was.

'Gone, teacher.'

'Gone where?'

'Turkey, teacher.'

It was the beginning of the great emigration.

≈

I was clearly getting used to Kabul—one night there was gunfire in the neighbourhood, a woman was murdered, and I slept right through it.

The Taliban launched their spring offensive in late May. You know, it's kind of like Spring Fashion Week, but kind of not. But what did this even mean? It wasn't as if they restricted themselves to a season for murdering, so why have a 'launch'? Did they have a theme for that year? Did they take advice from a PR company? Did they make sure they went to bed early before the big day? And what were their KPIs?

The day of the launch coincided with a concert Jennifer and I were giving at the house of one of her Afghan friends. We decided that this concert would be a counter-offensive with our own weapons—weapons of music. We had some trouble deciding whether we should call ourselves the Inshalladahs or the Khyber Passacaglia. We went with the Khyber Pass. The sun went down as we played Vivaldi in the garden, underneath pomegranate and mulberry trees. The audience of NGO workers and liberal Afghans lay on cushions and rugs on the grass, drinking Johnnie Walker Red Label. The evening had the feeling of a Gabriel Garcia Marquez novel, everything heightened and just outside the realm of credibility. This was only added to when I found out that Shoaib, Jennifer's friend, came from a family of nine brothers and one sister. And there was a copy of Plato's *Symposium* on top of the loo.

≈

After two months, the babies were coming along beautifully in their music garden. The cellists had been practising different rhythms, first of all playing air cello on their tummies, then on open strings. Jennifer and I used the Kodály method of rhythm words, a super simple and easy way to help a student say the correct rhythm. For these first rhythms, string players need to play quick notes using little bows, because that is the easiest way to control the bow at this stage.

Tikka tikka tee tee.

Tee tikka tee tikka.

Tikka tikka tikka tikka.

Around and around, again and again, the feeling slowly soaking into the fingers, the arm, the back, the brain.

The babies were also beginning to use their left hands, just lightly at first, with harmonics. One great pitfall at this point can be gripping the neck of the cello too hard, so to begin they touched the string just a little and learnt to hang off the fingerboard rather than press down onto it. Fatima did karate at the orphanage and her grip was astounding. Once gripping starts, it's very, very hard to cure.

The left hand on the cello essentially makes the same shape as the right hand with the bow—it's a C. If you have a glass handy, just pick it up with your left hand. Look at how your hand has fallen naturally, with your thumb vaguely opposite your rude (middle) finger, and your fingers curved around the glass. That's your left cello hand.

Hashi was doing pretty well with his bow hold, so we started on fingerboard hanging and, slowly, a D-major scale backwards. One morning I came in and he was all ready to go, his cello out, his bow rosined and him sitting staring out of the window, chewing the scroll of his cello. His bare, grubby toes were curled under him. I gave him some bread to chew instead of his cello, and we started our lesson.

～

Finally a minister of education was appointed, he signed my contract (personally) and I could now apply for a work visa.

I had to leave the country to re-enter on a bridging visa, which would then be transferred to a work visa. I took orders from the Mexicans for alcohol and IKEA, booked a fancy hotel, and went back to the twenty-first century.

Dubai was concrete and glitz, as opposed to concrete and dust, and I took the opportunity to swim and sleep and amble. It only took four days to get my visa, then I went back to Kabul. Back to a dangerous, dusty, aggressive, brutal place that was so full of love and beauty. My students were waiting for me with broad, relieved grins. Before I went the older ones had asked me if I was really coming back. Since a few foreign teachers had left abruptly, I understood why they were so worried. I had promised I would return, but they only believed me when they saw me in the flesh.

'We are your family now, Teacher Emma.'

'Teacher, I want to learn this!'

S ummer seeped into the walls of the city. The apple trees in
the Mexican House blossomed and the swallows continued
their mad circuits of the garden, joined now by a giant, prehis-
toric crow. The cries of the vegetable sellers in the street outside
changed from potatoes and onions to tomatoes and eggplants
and, moving on from the vegetable course, ice-cream. Young
boys pushed ice-cream wheelbarrows up and down the streets
of Kabul while a mechanical 'Happy Birthday to You!' squeezed
out of them like soft-serve on an Australian beach.

The open sewer outside our house began to fill with
maggots, and the roses now fought their beauty battle with
shit as well as guns and concrete. Shersha washed my sheets
and soaked them in sunlight to save my nose.

Now that I had my bridging visa, I needed to go and get a
work visa. Safi, one of the administrators from ANIM, collected

me one morning and we made our way over to the passport and visa office.

Although it was only 7 a.m., the whole street leading up to the passport office was packed. This was one of the few times I felt genuinely scared in Kabul; there were so many people, and a suicide bomber here would kill dozens and dozens. People walked along the street holding hope in their hands in the form of birth certificates, passport photos, proof-of-residence letters. Everyone was trying to leave and I was trying to stay.

I walked through security while a guard stabbed a man with a taser. This was going to be an interesting morning.

We wandered through a maze of administrative offices—seventies' buildings, prefabs, shipping containers and tiny alleyways. It felt like walking into the centre of an atom; everywhere, there was movement. Men, always men, with payraan tumbaan of all colours, various military uniforms, Western suits, pakols (Massoud the Civil War hero's hat of choice), karakuls (Karzai the previous president's hat of choice), turbans, skullcaps, and pattus (the Afghan shawl). The place was a catwalk, a demonstration of the different ways you could wear your pattu: swaddled like a baby, off the shoulder and casual like a movie star, or over your head and hidden away like Osama Bin Laden. After half an hour I followed the other foreigners to wait on a tiny staircase. Russians, Americans, Chinese, Indians, all with their fixer to guide them through this most advanced of bureaucratic challenges. Safi and I went into the office to have my form stamped; behind a massive desk sat a man who, judging by the decoration on his uniform, appeared to run the whole world. I greeted him with 'Salaam Aleikum' and, because of that, he gave me my visa that day.

~

Visa sorted, I could now open an account at the New Kabul Bank. This was the bank that processed army and government salaries from money largely donated by the good ol' US of A. The bank had risen from the ashes of the old Kabul Bank, after it went bust in a flurry of corrupt dealings; most of the US$1 billion that went missing in a black hole of dodgy loans has never been recovered. Now that the bank had been renamed, I was sure corruption was a thing of the past. Not.

The bank itself was certainly a thing of the past. Instead of automatic doors to greet you as you entered, there were automatic weapons. Instead of a smiling person asking you what service you required, there was a smiling person waiting to give you a body-search so intimate it really should have been preceded by dinner and a movie. I mean, she didn't even ask me my name. Instead of seeing one person and opening a bank account in twenty minutes, here I saw thirteen separate people and my bank account wouldn't be ready until a week later. One form was filled in after another; I was taken from one man to another, all of them young and bored and checking their Facebook. Women sat separated from men; the youthful helped the old. A medieval, detoothed man pressed his thumb on a pad of ink then onto a form as his son, blank-stared, held his hand.

~

I returned to school, to my Kabul normality. I walked past Professor Amruddin's room, just up the corridor from mine. Professor Amruddin taught the dilruba, a viol-like bowed instrument played sitting on the ground with it resting against your chest. The dilruba was an instrument nearly as ancient as Professor Amruddin. I would see him most mornings making his way very slowly to his room, wearing a white scarf and a karakul hat. He used a walking stick, as his body was at right angles to his legs, his shape from sitting to standing never changing. His face had no more room for wrinkles and his eyes had returned to the colour of a baby's—blue, opaque, with views of other worlds.

Professor Amruddin came from Kabul, but in the nineties he had had a music shop in Mazar-e-Sharif. The Taliban came, so he and his friends tried to save themselves by burying some instruments and burning others. They got rid of every single instrument in the shop except one: a dilruba given to Professor Amruddin by his father. This was the instrument he had wanted to keep forever. He took the strings off and all the decoration, hoping no one would recognise it as a musical instrument. A young boy did recognise it, though, at a checkpoint on the way to Herat. Perhaps the boy had once played the dilruba in his life before the Taliban. The boy took the instrument and smashed it against Professor Amruddin's car.

I looked in to Professor Amruddin's room. He was sitting on a cushion, his student Farhad, a boy with auburn hair, playing to him. Normally there is a certain amount of distance when a student plays to their teacher, but because Professor Amruddin was so old and so frail Farhad had sat himself directly in front of him, their feet nearly touching. It was a scene of delicate intimacy, this listening by a great musician to his future, to where his music would go.

~

News of ANIM's need for another small cello had spread far and wide, thanks to my friends John and Liz. I had thought if I could raise $1000 for a cello I'd be happy, but Liz and John had other ideas. They wrote to what seemed like everyone on their mailing lists, who wrote to their friends as well, and the $1000 was easily raised. The performing arts organisation Musica Viva in Australia helped by creating a fund, and within a couple of months these generous, kind Australians had raised over $20,000. That would be a lot of small cellos. In fact, Jennifer and I could really plan and set up the string department for good, with a range of small cellos, violins, violas, and even a half-sized double bass. ANIM would not need any more string instruments for years.

~

Just because I had a visa and a bank account, that didn't mean I would get paid any time soon. Jennifer lent me money for everyday things (there wasn't really anything else to buy) and I just had to wait. Wait for more forms to be signed, more men to drink tea, then eventually fill in even more forms. Wait and hope corruption didn't get to my salary before I did. I would maybe get paid in a couple of months. Maybe.

One thing I was really, really hanging out for was to get my own motorbike. When I had left Australia I had sold my beautiful Kristofer, a BMW F800GS. If you don't know this bike, it's the smaller version of the ones Ewan McGregor and Charley Boorman travelled from London to New York on in the TV series *Long Way Round*. Which makes it the coolest bike in the world. I knew I wouldn't be able to get anything quite like Kristofer, but the idea of riding around Kabul on any motorbike was dangerously, stupidly alluring. With a full-face helmet, Afghan shirt, jeans and boots, no one would know I was a woman, let alone a foreign woman. In anticipation I became a member of the Kabul Knights, Afghanistan's first motorbike club.

Riding in Kabul was a driving challenge almost beyond words. A Hieronymus Bosch painting might describe it better. I could say there were no road rules, but on closer observation that wasn't quite true. More that road rules were there if they didn't hold you back too much. As in most Asian countries, the general rule was to look after your front end. If everyone did that, in theory there wouldn't be any problem. In theory. In reality, Kabul drivers did U-turns abruptly on a four-lane highway, pulled out in front of you then braked sharply round a corner, dropped off passengers in the middle of the road and, most dangerous of all, drove the wrong way, frequently, down the middle of the street. Whoever had designed the road system of Kabul seemed to delight in the metaphor of roadblocks: just as the country as a whole was having a hard time getting anywhere, it was hard to get anywhere in Kabul without doing something illegal. Ironically, U-turns in Kabul were the only way to move forward.

One Friday I had my inaugural ride, out to the west of the city. I rode Jennifer's bike, an Iranian-made 150cc she had named Speedy Gonzales. The Speedy was removed, as Gonzales's top speed on the flat was fifty kilometres an hour. Jennifer was on the back of her German boyfriend Alex's bike. We rode out of town on Silo Road, a north–south artery with a wheat silo the Soviets had built for their army. Silo Road had been paved just a few weeks earlier—well, at least on one side. It had gone from a crater-filled, muddy roller-coaster to smooth bitumen heaven, but corruption had destroyed even this—the company who resurfaced the road had done a shoddy job and the government was so annoyed, they ripped the newly laid bitumen up again. Back to square one. For the rest of my time in Kabul, the best-built thing on Silo Road remained the silo.

We stopped first at an NGO named PARSA (Physiotherapy and Rehabilitation Services for Afghanistan). PARSA was run by an older American woman called Marnie, who had lived in Kabul in the 1960s and returned in 1996 to help develop the charity. It was based on a farm, and every Friday they held a brunch buffet for anyone who wanted to come. PARSA provided a vital meeting place for foreigners who worked outside of government restrictions; it became our second home, and Marnie our mother. The rock star Prince had quietly donated money to PARSA for years, and that money was used to build headquarters for the Scouts Association of Afghanistan. The scouts had been dib-dib-dibbing in Afghanistan for eighty years, only the Taliban had stopped them, and now Prince and Marnie had brought them back. After some food, our little biker gang gathered and we headed further west to Qargha Lake. The gang included Big Ben, a journalist, Courtney, another journalist on a scooter, Jake, a photographer who was having a break in Kabul from working in Syria (I guess safety is relative) on an Indian Enfield, and Chris and Alyssa, our Übermensch Vikings. Chris had been a commando and had the body of a Greek god with the beard of an imam, and Alyssa would have turned heads anywhere, let alone Kabul. She was six foot, with long, curly, flaming-red hair.

The Paghman River was dammed in 1933 to create Qargha Lake. The lake was one of the most popular places to visit outside Kabul on a Friday, with people taking picnics, going fishing, just doing normal things. The Taliban had attacked a hotel on the lake in 2012 and twenty-four people were killed. People killed, just doing normal things.

Our little biker gang attracted serious attention as we rode out past Qargha to Paghman village. The traffic became worse and worse, with young men yelling at us from their cars and hassling Courtney, with her more obvious female figure, in particular. We decided to head home and I got stuck behind a police pick-up truck with rocket launchers sticking out of the back. There might not have been many road rules in Kabul, but one internationally accepted rule in this circumstance was STFB: stay the fuck back.

~

When Jennifer and I arrived back at the Mexican House, Elias, one of the young boys next door, met us and kissed our hands. I'm not sure I'd ever had my hand kissed in greeting before, and certainly not by a five-year-old. Elias had a deep scar running from the top of his nose to his mouth, which gave him the look of a baby Mafioso. I felt a rush of compassion between us, a bond of humanity. Such an adult action from a wounded child. Elias then proceeded to run upstairs and throw stones at Nacho from the roof.

Bibi limped out, her leg still in a splint, and invited us in for tea. I was still her son. Conversation stumbled along in a not-speaking-each-other's-language-much way until Jennifer said that we needed to go to the vet as her cat had a bad eye. Bibi looked confused and a little embarrassed, turned to her daughter and they both laughed hysterically. Apparently the phrase 'having a bad eye' means something else in Dari; what Jennifer had actually said was that we needed to go the vet because her cat was a womaniser.

What must they have thought of us?

~

After weeks and weeks of having to be driven around, the euphoria of riding a bike again, at least on Fridays, was huge. I started to actually feel at home in Kabul. I returned to school with renewed enthusiasm, even if, as the term drew to a close, the school itself seemed to be going through an unenthusiastic phase. I had not experienced the type of group mentality in other schools that I did at ANIM; the mood swings were ferocious. One day the school would be steady, almost peaceful, then the collective mood would swing to petulance and savagery. Students would hit each other and shout and sulk in class. On days like these, it seemed like nobody learnt anything and all we could do was wait. Again.

The teenage girls in particular were *so* moody. Wow. Coming back to Kabul from Dubai, I had met a South African who, when he heard where I was teaching, said, 'You're brave!'

I thought he was talking about the lack of effective security at the school and I started to dissemble, saying it was fine. He interrupted me and said how brave I was teaching teenage girls.

Many of the girls lived together in the 'orphanage' and clearly picked up on each other's hormonal variations. They tore into each other verbally, hit each other, stared the stare of a true monster, and then would suddenly break into an exquisite, disarming smile.

'Girls, be kind to each other,' I beseeched them.

Something had to be done.

I had been practising Vipassana meditation for about two years and, even though I wasn't the slightest bit qualified to teach the technique to the girls, I could at least give a simple introduction to meditating on their breath. I asked Dr Sarmast if I could introduce meditation in the girls' ensemble and he was delighted with the idea. I checked with Allegra and in the next rehearsal we began.

For young people who live in a world where they are hardly ever alone and where the culture is one of constant chatter, meditating was always going to be a prodigious challenge.

With Laila's help in translating, I asked the girls to put their instruments on the floor and to close their eyes. Giggle giggle. Then I asked them to focus on their breath. Giggle giggle, mutter mutter. Then I asked them to push any thoughts away like balloons and come back to the feeling of the breath in their nose. Giggle giggle, snigger. And then we entered a world of silence.

I started them off with just three minutes. Three minutes of stillness in Kabul, where there is never, ever stillness, was three lifetimes long. Some girls smirked, some talked, some tried to play their instruments, but enough took it seriously that their influence held sway. The girls came out of their meditation with different looks on their faces, softer and kinder. We did meditation at every rehearsal after that and the girls even started to ask for it. The mood was always less intense and fractious afterwards.

The ensemble was rehearsing a new 'Women's Song' written by Ustad Shefta. It was to be broadcast on TV all around Afghanistan, with Negin conducting. It would be a huge event and so important for women and men all around the country to see how brilliant these girls were. After the rehearsal, Negin raced up to me; she had Daniel Barenboim and the West–Eastern Divan Orchestra's boxed set of Beethoven symphonies in her hand, a donation from the library upstairs.

'Teacher, look! This is what I will listen to tomorrow!'

'Hey, cool, Negin. Let me know which is your favourite.'

Then, on Saturday morning: 'Teacher, number three. No! Number nine. No. Number six! Oh, I don't know . . . They are all *so* great!'

~

Besides Dr Sarmast, there was one local teacher who was outstanding in his commitment to the school: Ustad Wali, the English program co-ordinator. The US embassy funded the program and he had set up a comprehensive course for the students. Wali had special projects for different celebrations, such as Teachers' Day or Children's Day, and he was always joyful, attentive, lively and smartly dressed. If one of the foreign teachers said something dismissive about Afghanistan, he would question what they meant, and why they were being rude about his country. It was certainly easy to be dismissive of Afghanistan, so I appreciated Wali's righteous passion. Many students like Negin, Laila and Shaperai also showed great work ethic, but the junior staff were becoming increasingly lackadaisical.

I had the most to do with Fayez, the violin teacher. When I had taught him on my previous trips, Fayez had always seemed impressively surly. Of course he had every right to be surly, but at some point, when other students had grown up and cheered up, Fayez had not. He had many things to be grateful for: he was Jennifer's assistant and she was the most dynamic violin teacher I had ever met. He was being paid by ANIM and also earned money from outside gigs. He was the best violinist in the country. Yet he was obviously very, very pissed off with his lot in life. Jennifer did her best to teach him not only how to teach, but how to appreciate his life. It never did any good. This left me with the suspicion that the things of value that I wanted to work on with these students—moral choices, larger philosophical concepts, the stuff I felt was just as important as learning music, if not more so—were impossible to discuss, partly because of my inadequate language skills but also because the students had no room for it. Their lives were just too hard. Why think about difficult stuff if you can laugh and joke around instead?

The other junior teachers did just enough work to keep their jobs, but most days I saw them sitting around in the hallway looking at their Facebook feeds, chatting. Always chatting. If Afghanistan could have been rebuilt by gossip, it would have been a fully developed nation in a year.

Shaheer, our assistant housekeeper and the junior theory teacher, was a particularly sad example of this hopelessness. He had so many skills: not only could he play trumpet and trombone reasonably well, but he was also very talented at fixing wind instruments. And he was a beautiful teacher, especially with the younger students. Jennifer, Cami, Allegra and I all tried to help Shaheer as much as possible. Cami suggested he start up an instrument repair shop and make music stands to sell to ANIM and army bands (all our stands were imported and they were continually breaking). Shaheer sat there, glum and aggressive, and said that he wanted to go to Germany with a people smuggler. We tried desperately to get him to see it wouldn't work. Even if he survived the journey (we were starting to read horrific reports of people drowning in the Mediterranean) he would probably not gain refugee status. He wasn't Hazara, he wasn't oppressed, he had two jobs. Shaheer became more and more depressed and we simply could not do anything for him. He started to say he just needed somewhere quiet and peaceful.

God. Everybody did.

～

The baby cellists' playing grew every week. Pedran, the smart, haughty boy, was simply exceptional. He played his harmonics lightly and cleanly, hung off the fingerboard like a monkey, played a D-major scale backwards with tikka tikka tee tee, and then rolled his eyes at me; it was clearly time for 'Twinkle, Twinkle, Little Star'.

It feels like the equivalent of watching your child walk for the first time when your student plays their first 'Twinkle'. It is the culmination of many weeks, sometimes months, of work. Often, from this moment, the student will really start to fly with their playing. It is probably also the biggest leap they will ever make in development, from only playing open strings and a little scale to playing their very first tune.

Pedran played the first line with great confidence and style, as though he'd been playing for twenty years. The other students were all different: Meena with grace, care and love; Hashi, plucking, because the poor little chap had broken his thumb; Fatima with shyness and faux indifference, but ultimately joy that she had managed to do it. So, with the difficult part over, it would be downhill now to the Dvorak Concerto.

∼

The babies were a delight, a daily reminder of my purpose in Kabul. The joy and the horror of Afghanistan became a palimpsest of feelings: you scratched one and bits of the other would be revealed. One didn't seem to even exist without the other; they lay entwined, symbiotic, unavoidable.

There were awful days when security became a serious worry. As the Taliban began to warm up after their spring offensive announcement, they attacked a guesthouse where foreign teachers at ANIM had stayed in the past. Fourteen people were killed. Then two attacks on government buses, one attack at the university, another at the airport, frequent cutting of the Internet. The Taliban were probably meeting their KPIs. Even foreigners who had been there for years were saying how bad things were getting. Some began to talk about getting a gun, but it was surprisingly hard to; it would have been much easier in the States. We discussed the idea at the Mexican House, as having a rifle in your own home was legal without a licence. Chris, the Übermensch ex-commando, advised us against it.

'Have you ever used a gun?'

Me: 'No.'

'Have you had any training at all in weaponry?'

'Er, no.' I figured playing the viola didn't count.

'Have you seen what happens to someone when they are shot at close range?'

'No. Gosh, no.'

'Then don't get a gun. Things only ever get worse with guns.'

The worsening security meant our life was severely curtailed in terms of how, where and when we travelled. No boozing or pool parties at the US embassy. Relaxing on Fridays became a very quiet affair of yoga, headbutting Nacho and watching *Game of Thrones*. Jennifer bought a paddling pool, so we sat in it in the garden drinking whisky and Coke, laughing hysterically at everything.

I needed something, someone. I needed a light to tell me all these constraints and risks were worth it. Someone extraordinary. Someone who I could teach the most important things to, not just how to play the cello.

And then Atesh came.

Atesh was like an Afghan puppy—short brown hair, green eyes, limbs not quite grown into, a little beyond conscious control. Atesh played the piano and had grown up in Pakistan before his parents decided to return to Kabul. He was called Atesh, meaning fire, because his mother wanted him to set the world alight.

Atesh came into my room one lunchtime. I had met him before, but we had only had little chats up till then as I didn't teach any classes to him.

'Teacher Emma, I want to learn the cello. Do you have time to teach me?'

And that is how our lessons began.

Over the weeks and months, Atesh told me more about his life. His family had moved to Pakistan during the civil war.

Because they were so poor, his parents made the harrowing decision to put Atesh into an orphanage, so he could receive better food. He stayed in the orphanage for four years. His parents used the time to study English and computers, but Atesh saw them regularly and, once his father started working, he was able to go and live with them again. Atesh was so scared to return to Afghanistan. In Pakistan Atesh was happy, but he couldn't speak Dari or Pashtu well, so the thought of returning to his mother country without his mother language was very confronting. But then Atesh came to ANIM. Dr Sarmast had to fight hard for Atesh to attend, as he entered the school later than other students (much like Laila). AFCECO, the orphanage/hostel, helped Atesh by giving him Dari lessons and advocating with Dr Sarmast to gain a place for him. Just like Laila, Atesh worked hard, so hard, to catch up to his classmates. For the previous two years he had been class valedictorian.

Atesh's mum was initially doubtful about him studying music, but eventually she saw how much change music could bring. His parents were unusual in Afghanistan: they chose to only have two children (Atesh had a younger sister) and his father listened to Western classical music. He had shown Atesh the film *The Pianist* when Atesh was young, and, since he saw how his son was drawn to music and the piano in particular, he played Atesh as many films and as much music as he could find. Atesh made the point to me that the pianist survived the Second World War because he was a musician; in Afghanistan's war, being a musician would mean certain death.

Atesh was extremely intelligent. More than intelligent, he was constantly seeking explanations, searching for links, comparisons, opposites, apposites, anything to make sense of his world. And not just in music. Atesh spoke fluent English, as he had gone to an English-medium school in Pakistan, so there was no limit to the subjects we covered in our lessons. Perhaps the only slight problem was that the cello didn't get played as often as I would have liked.

Atesh came to my room whenever he could. We sat together and listened to all types of music: John Cage, Philip Glass, Mahler, Bach, jazz. He listened without prejudice or knowledge, which meant he asked endless questions.

'Teacher Emma, why does Mahler write such long pieces?'

'Is it hard to play Glass? How do you not get lost?'

'Why did Cage write silence? Did he need to?'

I began to spend more time with Atesh than any other student. He would greet me in the morning, hang out at break and lunchtime, then come and say goodbye after school. Atesh became my light.

～

In many ways, ANIM was extraordinary: a music school in a war-torn city. A school of street kids and middle-class kids, students with no family, students with a family that had no end. A school that fought for its existence every day, a school that had become one of the very few beacons of hope in Afghanistan. But ANIM was also just a regular school. And regular schools had parent–teacher days.

Dr Sarmast announced that there would be a parent–teacher meeting for the whole school the following Saturday. From previous Australian and English experiences, I had expected the parents to come in with their children and talk to each teacher individually about their child's progress. That way, if there was anything negative to be discussed, it could be done in private. This was not to be the case.

At 8 a.m., parents and teachers crowded into the staffroom. I had put on my fanciest clothes (an embroidered Indian dress) and even I was surprised by how feminine I looked. We teachers sat facing the parents, all divided by gender, women at the front. Some of the women wore burqas, with the mesh screen pulled back over the top of their head, which looked kind of natty. Some wore modern dress with minimal hijab, very stylish. One woman, actually Hafizah's mum, wore the niqab, a black veil with a tiny slit, so I could only see her eyes. Some of the women wore plastic shoes; some had expensive high heels. All of them had hands that had worked—big, wide, strong hands that had held children, wrung laundry, scrubbed houses, kneaded dough. These women all had an air of defiant patience.

The meeting began with a prayer sung by the Islamic teacher; he was standing right behind me and I could feel the vibrations of his belief in my chest.

Each teacher talked about each child in great detail. As you can imagine, it took a long time. The parents, particularly the fathers, showed a mix of awe and respect for Dr Sarmast, but eventually slight boredom as yet another child was talked about at length in front of everyone. I tried to shorten things a little by simply saying all my students were fine, and thanked their parents for sending them to the school. It didn't really help much.

After nearly four hours of discussing each student, and how bad the school lunches were, we all had tea and cake. It was such an everyday, simple meeting of all these people, and I kept thinking how this could never have happened during the Taliban years.

I met Laila and Hafizah's mums. The two were contrasting in their dress, but not their actions—while Hafizah's mum wore a niqab, Laila's mum wore a pretty, embroidered hijab, her face open to the world. She had fought for her daughter to go to school, fought against the rest of her family. Hafizah's mum had fought as well, but she came from a much more conservative background. We talked through a translator, one of the English teachers. I said how great Hafizah was, such a good student, how the school wasn't the same when she was away and how I hoped she would get better soon, after another period away.

'Thank you for giving my daughter the education I could never have.' And her mum's eyes receded again within their veil.

Sonam stood waiting to talk to me—an old woman, her mother, holding her hand. Sonam's body had thickened in recent weeks, and she had missed nearly every viola lesson. Sonam, it seemed, had signed out. When she did turn up, she had shown zero interest in the viola, and I was becoming increasingly frustrated with her.

I smiled at her mother and said what a good student Sonam was, but that I was worried as she had missed so many lessons. Sonam's mum looked on, her eyes flitting from side to side, her burqa pushed up onto her forehead. She was a widow in one of the hardest places in the world to be a widow. She had a family to support, and if one of those children could find a good match, it would have been a relief of enormous significance. Her mother looked ashamed, embarrassed, and said that Sonam was getting married, so she had many things to prepare—which included being fattened up for the wedding. Sonam said her husband would come to live in Kabul, so that she could still come to school.

'Education first, teacher!'

That was the last time I saw Sonam.

Heat now soaked the very foundations of the city. Summer began to melt Kabul from the inside out, a heat that should have melted even the gun barrels. Lenti-two the tortoise, perhaps needing a drink, reappeared from a long absence, only to race off somewhere else again. Shersha made some long, loose shirts for me, but I knew I was lucky: so many Afghan women wore the same clothes in summer as in winter—trousers, long shirts, a long coat, hijab. And then maybe a burqa to finish the ensemble off, or finish the woman off.

The air was leadenly still, then in the afternoons a wind would come in off the Hindu Kush that whipped up all the dust in the city. We had had poop rain; now we had poop dust. The wind was so strong that flights were cancelled nearly every day. Jennifer was due to go for a holiday, but wept as her flight was delayed. The smallest inconvenience could send any one of us into a tailspin. I observed my own mood beginning to swing ferociously, just like the students; it seemed there was no equilibrium to be had. The only person who remained calm was Allegra, but she had migraines nearly every Friday. The stress came out in us all, just in different ways.

Since many of the students didn't have easy access to water, they weren't able to wash every day. This, on top of having only one uniform for the entire six-day week, meant the smells in school were becoming a tad potent. One day after school I was coaching a quartet of teenage girls, playing an arrangement of the traditional standard 'French Folk Song'. The window and door were open, but these girls smelt as I remembered my own teenage smell from a particular time of the month. Dr Sarmast walked in and promptly walked out again.

'Ms Ayres, you deserve a medal.'

I was conducting the girls, but they had other ideas; they all wanted to try conducting for themselves. One by one they came and joined me to practise. First Samia, neat and precise. Then Cevinch, wild and masterful. Sombal joined in, hesitant and giggly, then Shaperai, determined not to be left out. In the end I had four girls conducting with wildly different beats and me playing a quarter-size violin, trying to be diplomatic and follow them all. These young girls all wanted to have a say in how their world sounded, what speed it should go; they wanted to be dominant for once in their lives. And, even though they were only conducting one player, it was a moment of power. It was a perfect metaphor for Afghanistan: President Ghani and Abdullah Abdullah, the chief executive of the country, fighting each other instead of leading; everybody wanting to have their own say; no one really listening to each other. And me, as a metaphor for the outside world, without a clue what to do except play along.

Just when summer could not get any hotter, the fasting month of Ramadan started. Muslims were forbidden from eating or drinking from about 3 a.m. to 7.30 p.m. Jennifer and I began Ramadan with enormous determination, thrilled to be joining our Afghan friends and students. Hafizah found out I was fasting and asked if I was Muslim. I said no, I was Christian. I had learnt it was much better to say you were Christian than to admit no faith at all; people in this country, which defied belief, couldn't understand anyone who had no belief. Hafizah smiled beatifically at me and said, 'Teacher Emma, you are welcome to Islam!'

I lasted three days. But in those three days, I felt the beauty and power of this religion like never before. I had a glimpse of how it gave you a chance to look deep inside and assess your own commitment, how it bonded you with God and with your fellow Muslims. How the whole of the city, the country, the Muslim world, was breaking fast together. How a thick, soft silence descended over the city as the muezzins called to stop eating. And how it delivered a burden too heavy for some—my baby viola student Omran had started fasting even though he hadn't reached puberty yet. As each day went on, Omran, already skinny, became wan and weak, eyes on stalks. We had a lesson in sitting as he was simply too weak to stand.

It was nearly forty degrees Celsius during the day. Even Nacho was hot, although, looking at the roses, clearly not fasting. I went on a reduced fast from 6 a.m. to 7 p.m. I couldn't think, do yoga, do anything useful except watch *Game of Thrones*. Even this was too much, so I moved to a WWF—Weak Westerner Fast—sneaking water when no one was looking, eating breakfast around 2 p.m.

Just when Ramadan could not get any harder, term exams began. I had watched the students become increasingly sallow as Ramadan went on; many of these young people were in a dubious state of health to begin with anyway, and now they had exams to deal with as well. Did their stresses never end?

Exams began each morning at 7.30 and were supposed to finish at midday. This rarely happened and I felt most sorry for the students taking their instrumental exams late in the day. One poor clarinettist, Mohsin, hardly made any sound at all as he virtually mimed his way through his scales.

Listening to little kids play music has to be one of the greatest pleasures in the world. Hearing a well-known piece reconstructed or deconstructed, played in surprising rhythms (otherwise known as 'wrong'), is infinitely wonderful. For two weeks I listened to oboe, violin, guitar, viola, cello, double bass, clarinet, piano, saxophone, percussion, trumpet, French horn and flute exams. I listened to scales in major, natural minor, melodic minor and harmonic minor forms (and sometimes was not quite able to tell the difference), I listened to ensemble pieces, I listened to a girl play Bach on the piano and sing harmony at the same time (very Glenn Gould), I listened to rudimentary playing and I heard some truly beautiful music making. All these kids were musicians, and I wished a TV news film crew could have been there to send it out to the world. *This* was Afghanistan as well.

Nazira, my best student, was better able to keep up her cello practice as, for unknown reasons, she wasn't observing Ramadan.

Nazira looked like a tiny supermodel. She had blonde hair and blue-green eyes, cheekbones of alabaster and a quiet, secret smile, like she had come from another world and only returned to earth to remind herself how simple humankind was. She had come to me at the beginning of term with a piece of sheet music in her hand.

'Teacher, I want to learn this!'

It was a copy of J.S. Bach's first cello suite, the prelude. The one that, whenever anyone hears it, they say how much they would like to play the cello.

I was in a dilemma: the piece was a little too hard for Nazira, but she desperately wanted to play it and would therefore practise it a lot. I decided to let her, and she blossomed like the roses on the streets. I have never seen anyone improve so much in such a short time. She played the prelude in her exam and the examiners burst into spontaneous applause. Nazira looked over to me, smiled her secret smile, and ran from the room. She knew that she had gone through the gates of cello heaven with that piece. There was no return.

The baby strings played a mini concert for visitors from the World Bank and, since time was short, we also made that performance their exam. They were superb. They performed 'Twinkle, Twinkle, Little Star' in four-part harmony; all fourteen of them had excellent posture, bow holds, left-hand position and tone. The World Bank people were dumbfounded.

'How long have they been playing?'

'Three months.'

'I simply cannot believe it.'

Dr Sarmast stood to the side, bursting with pride. It was a glorious moment. Afterwards we sat together and sang Afghan songs. Rohullah, a little viola player, sang on his own, his high voice reaching up into the air like a shaft of light, all the emotion of his country's history distilled in that young voice.

I stepped back into the Western world for two weeks, visiting my mum and sister, Liz, in England. Liz and I went to London, cycled, drank Guinness, ate what must have added up to a whole pig, and then it was time to go back to what was now my home. I was itching to return, to get back on that Kabul joy/terror ride.

I had missed all my students, but particularly Laila and Atesh. Laila had played extremely well in her exam; her tone had improved and deepened, and she was learning to shift to different positions on the viola fingerboard. All this without any family support or practice outside school. I was looking forward to carrying on our lessons and beginning a whole new viola book with her.

School term began again and a kerfuffle of students stood waiting for me in my room. Baby viola players, baby cellists, big cellists with secret smiles, a new chap called Sultan who wanted to start double bass, Amruddin with his rockabilly hair, but no Laila.

'Does anyone know where Laila is?'

I dreaded the answer. After all this, would she join the missing girls?

'Gone, teacher.'

'Gone where?'

7

A prison of music

It was raining outside. It may have been only August, but autumn was sending advance notice of the dying to come, with smells of rotting leaves and night chills. It had been raining all night, so Nacho would have a little bloat from eating wet rose petals. I'd looked up how to cure mild bloat: hold the stomach from underneath and gently lift until the goat starts to belch. Do not stand in front of the goat's mouth. Or, indeed, behind the goat's bottom.

Laila had gone and Pedran had gone too. Jennifer told me on the day of Pedran's lesson. We were due to work on a new piece and Pedran was going to be amazing at it. He was going to look at me with a smile and a scowl, through his one-lens glasses, and play his new piece perfectly straight away. He was going to make a pure, strong sound then roll his eyes until I gave him something harder. But Pedran had gone with his family to France. His father, an architect, had been given a visa. I was devastated; I was delighted. I imagined the little chap in twenty years speaking French, dressed elegantly, playing the Dvorak Cello Concerto with the Orchestre de Paris. Pedran and his family had escaped this disastrous country and a little part of me wanted him back. Maybe in France he would get a new lens for his glasses.

School swung back into its particularly Afghan rhythm: an uneven, capricious rhythm of sudden pointless meetings, missing students with no reason given, the babies moving on to new songs and quartets, Nazira demanding harder and harder pieces, Shaperai practising relentlessly, Hafizah returning to her usual gossiping joy. Order and chaos, hand in hand.

My ear-training classes were a little more successful than the previous term. The grade twelve boys had become used to me, and me to them; we listened to Gloria Estefan in their lesson, Ahmad and Mustaffah playing air tabla with their fingers swirling around their faces. The boys came to me afterwards with their virus-laden USB drives, asking for 'the happy music'.

I had started to use the teaching method of listening to a lot of music, plus added stories, with the grade elevens.

One Thursday I played them Thomas Tallis's *Spem in Alium* (if you haven't heard this piece then stop reading and download it *now*). The work is for forty voices a cappella, written at a time when women in Europe were still burned at the stake for heresy and witchcraft. In Afghanistan, this was no distant memory. *Spem in Alium* is an extended aural nirvana, a musical refuge. The students were being a bit rowdy so I played it to calm them down.

'How many parts are there?' I asked.

'Three, four—no, five!' they all shouted.

'What are the instruments?'

'Oboe! Violin!'

'The voice of a human!'

'What was it written for?'

'The church, teacher?'

'Yes, the church, but only voices, and there are forty parts.'

They couldn't believe it.

'Do you like it?'

'YES!'

'Why do you like it?'

'The sound, teacher, the sound. It is *so* beautiful.'

The expressions on their exquisite Afghan faces showed their truth.

At that point, and with the babies, with Nazira, with Gloria Estefan, with Atesh, it was always about the music. Nothing could better it. Music became, more than ever before, my friend, my teacher, my shelter, my priest, my confessor and my counsel.

On 19 March 2015, a woman dressed in a black chador and niqab left work and walked to a mosque in the centre of Kabul to pray. It was rush hour, two days before the Shia new year festival of Nowruz; traffic laboured past the woman along the potholed road by the filthy river. Market stalls lined the road, and men, with very few women, strolled along buying clothes,

vegetables, dried fruit. The woman worked as a religious studies teacher. She was young and deeply devout. She had just finished a degree in religious studies, had memorised the Koran, and was planning to start a family. After her prayers she was going to go home to help her mother decorate for Nowruz.

She stopped by the entrance to the mosque and spoke to a mullah, who was selling amulets. She questioned why he was degrading the mosque by selling things in this religious place, and he, perhaps embarrassed and angry at being told off by a woman, perhaps stressed about the coming new year celebrations and not having enough money to enjoy them, perhaps frustrated by years of war and lack of education, he, this religious servant of God, shouted out a sentence that meant that the woman would be dead within an hour. And killed in the grimmest way imaginable. The woman's name was Farkhunda Malikzada.

Farkhunda cowered in a corner of the entrance as the mullah berated her, drawing more and more men to the scene. The mullah accused Farkhunda of burning the Koran, producing one from a nearby bin. Despite her cries of innocence (and her actual innocence), she was beaten, stripped of her veil, kicked in the face, and stamped on. Men stood around, holding up their mobile phones to video her assault. There was a moment of stillness after the first beatings, during which Farkhunda is left sitting on the ground, her veil torn off, a plastic shoe discarded, her eyes searching for comprehension. In stark contrast to her previously neat hijab, now her hair raged around her face and blood smeared her skin, a macabre version of a mudpack.

A few policemen arrived and tried to defend her, shooting their pistols into the air. The mob pleaded with the policemen to let them have Farkhunda. Two policemen, in desperation, dragged her up on top of the shrine, a corrugated-iron roof with a steep pitch, but they couldn't keep hold of her. A man reached up with a long metal pole and swiped at Farkhunda, knocking her back to the ground, to the mob below. She managed to stand up for a brief moment as blows of wood and steel rained down on her, but the man with the pole hit her again and she fell for the last time. She was beaten with the pole, with planks of wood, with feet and hands, until, mercifully unconscious, she was dragged by a car for two hundred metres, thrown in a riverbed and burned. Her clothes were so soaked with her blood that her attackers had to use their own scarves to get her body to catch fire. It took effort. It all took so much effort, but was done so easily, in view of the police. In the hour the mob took to kill Farkhunda, police reinforcements could have arrived. They didn't. Nothing was done. Nobody saved her. Farkhunda, now only her body, was left to burn in the dried-up riverbed, amongst the rubbish and stray dogs.

～

'Teacher Emma, I have something to show you. Do you have time?'

It had been a calm morning and I had caught up with all my work, so I beckoned Atesh to take a seat on the floor next to me. He opened his computer to his music-notation software and played me his new piece.

It was called 'Farkhunda—In Memorium'.

I had still been in Australia when Farkhunda Malikzada was murdered. I had assumed that the mob must have been made up of older men, men whom society was passing by, men who had grown up in the Taliban era and who couldn't make the changes necessary to survive in slightly more progressive Kabul.

But when I read reports of the murder, and forced myself to watch the video, I saw for myself that this was not the case. The men were not very old, not even in middle age; in fact, most of them were young, teenagers or barely older, dressed in jeans and football shirts, with fashionable haircuts that belied their barbarity. What puzzled me was that most of the men who murdered Farkhunda would have grown up in relative peace, during the post-Taliban Coalition years. They should have had better access to schools, healthcare, jobs and hope than their parents and grandparents. On 19 March 2015, this was shown to be savagely untrue. What was shown to be savagely true was that there was a monstrous anger in Afghanistan towards invasion, lack of progress, unemployment, increasing violence, corruption and troop withdrawal, and Farkhunda Malikzada became the people's object of revenge.

Many of these young, beautiful murderers could have been the boy-men whom I taught. So many times the grade twelves had stood in front of me, scratching their crotches and being subtly intimidating, and I had tried to ignore it. After watching the video of Farkhunda, a warning came crashing down and I barked at them to leave. It would have been so easy to think of every young Afghan man in this way, so when Atesh came with his piece for the memory of Farkhunda, he saved me from this shallow mindset.

'Teacher Emma, when I heard about Farkhunda I cried a lot. I was scared. I didn't believe it at first. Now, I can't get it out of my mind. If justice is not served for her, it will keep on happening. Maybe people will even attack our school. So, how could I help? I'm trying not to forget Farkhunda, with my music.'

Atesh sat beside me, discussing the different lines of his piece, his green eyes wet with tears for Farkhunda. The music was written for a string quartet, a simple, meandering tune with pizzicato accompaniment. It was perfect.

Sama and Parwana were the administrative staff at school, and both in their early thirties. When I asked Sama if she was married, she said, 'No! Thanks to God!'

Sama was small and elegant, and if she had been born in a different country would have gone to Oxford or Harvard. Nevertheless, Sama had an Afghan degree and was planning to go to India to take a Masters in Business Studies. She was extraordinarily organised and when Dr Sarmast was away she ran the school. The male teachers criticised her for being outspoken and bossy, in a milder version of Farkhunda's fate. They learnt to hold their tongues and stuck to gossiping behind her back.

As with so many of the women in Afghanistan, Sama and Parwana couldn't exercise (although they did all the cleaning, which must have been exercise enough). When I talked with them about yoga, they said they wanted to try it, so after school one day we shut ourselves in Dr Sarmast's office, along with Jennifer and Allegra. In a moment of what seemed the most extreme intimacy, Sama and Parwana took off their hijabs and we began. Breathing first—I explained the internal breathing locks (core and women's 'bits'—lots of giggles) and we headed into some postures. Sama was small and round and dived into downward-facing dog pose like an ancient yogi, flexible and committed. Just as we were starting trikonasana, which involves holding your big toe from the side and looking up at your outstretched hand, the man in charge of the Internet, Bakhtiari, walked into the office. His seeing us all without our headscarves was the equivalent of seeing us in just our underwear. Yoga would have to go on the list of things to wait for.

Laila was waiting for me one Saturday morning, three weeks after she had gone. She was standing outside my room and ran to me as I walked down the corridor. I was overwhelmed, I was mad. I had tried to not be upset about Laila disappearing, but how could I not be? She had come back and I felt like a child had returned. I was also mad because she had not said anything about going and didn't really explain herself. I had the now familiar feeling that I was living inside *One Thousand and One Nights*, with every day a new story being told, an Afghan truth being created.

Laila hedged around the subject, giving only little bits of vague information. Her expression receded inwards as she decided what to tell, what to keep. She was defiant, almost rude, more determined, more fickle, less reliable, less magnificent.

This country ripped the guts out of people. Here I found more and more that the truth was something moveable, fluid. There was only the truth that people told you. And then you found another version, from another person. Shabheer, Allegra's husband, said that Afghans don't tell the truth because truth hurts you more than a lie.

Laila's grandmother lived in Quetta, just over the border in Pakistan from Kandahar, and home to hundreds of thousands of Hazara refugees. Her grandmother wanted her to marry, or maybe she wanted Laila to look after her because she was sick. Other students said that Laila's grandmother wasn't sick but that Laila had tried to stay in Pakistan. All I knew was that I would never know the truth, and maybe Laila wouldn't either.

We returned to our music lessons. Laila was preparing for a recital of the first Suzuki book. We played duets and her tone was massive, the music shining through. Students and teachers would wander into our room, drawn by the beauty of Laila's sound. We talked about finding the joy in music, rather than being worried about whether it was correct or not; her approach to music had been mirroring her own stresses with her family. With this one simple idea, her playing was transformed and her music smiled.

Looking back on this time, I wonder whether Laila disappearing was the first chink in the wall of my belief in the school, in Afghanistan's bright future. It was a simple reminder that no matter what I did, Laila could, would, disappear at any moment.

It was break time. Rohullah, the boy with the singing voice of an angel who has seen hell, ran up the stairs beside me. Rohullah always looked scared, with dark rings under his eyes. He had the twisted body of an old man wrapped in a child's skin.

'Teacher Emma, I can play sol major!'

'Wow, Rohullah, that's great! How many sharps in sol major?'

'One, teacher, fa sharp.'

'Yes! How many sharps in re major?'

'Two, teacher! Fa and do!'

None of the other babies liked Rohullah. They called him *deewana*, crazy, and pulled faces behind his back. The only way Rohullah was going to make progress in this country was to play his way out. He ran off, his skinny knee poking out of the hole in his trousers, the viola by his side his only friend.

Hafizah had come back after the school break looking fatter and healthier. Her mother was recovering from her head injury and her brother from his motorbike crash. She came to help with the babies' group sessions and, as she persuaded their little hands to go into the correct shapes on their cellos, she showed a patience and kindness not always evident in her.

141

At break time Hafizah danced down the corridor, enticing girls and boys to follow her, to gossip with her, to engage in exactly that moment fully. If I had been a student at the school, I would have wanted to be friends with Hafizah. She was where the party was at, although her vivacity never really extended to cello practice. She only did the bare minimum, just enough to make slow progress through a piece. Hafizah's talents and heart lay in seducing people with conversation, not with music. I watched as she moved down the corridor, whispering in a girl's ear here, slapping a boy across the back there, playing with the babies, never studying. I felt Hafizah had the power to change Afghanistan, if only she would study a little.

Hafizah had missed a lesson.

'Sick, teacher,' was the reply from her friend Samia.

I feared that Hafizah's blood pressure and stress problems had come back. I saw her the next day, crying with Samia by the metal blast door. Her gaunt face had returned, this time filled with pain. She could hardly move. As I approached, the girls stiffened, closing ranks.

'Hafizah, what happened? Are you okay?'

'Nothing, teacher, just my neck is bad.'

Jennifer found out that Hafizah's brother, now that he had recovered from his bike crash, had felt well enough to beat Hafizah for not looking after him better. He had punched her in the neck so much she couldn't move her head for a week.

≈

In Afghanistan, violence was not confined to the Taliban. I began to understand how it was encoded into everyone's life here. Even the land itself was violent: there were minor earth tremors every few days, shaking the Mexican House enough for sweet Cami to wake us up and make sure we were not scared.

There were so many things I could have been, often was, scared of—the tremors, the Taliban, kidnapping gangs, the traffic, Dr Sarmast, the resentful Afghan teachers, the hopeless junior staff, the angry kids. Being scared became a background noise for me, one I blended into my life until I only noticed it when I was going to school, or when a bomb blast surged from a distance.

Despite the ocean of smiles, the laughter, the glee at school, there was always a feeling that violence was not far away—the angry look, the swipe at a friend, the snatch of an instrument, swift bullets for words. I had a young man called Shoaib for music theory. He was always very polite, charming even, again with a disarming smile and a graciousness that few men in the West could ever muster. Shoaib had an argument with a teacher, the sergeant major teacher, who told him he shouldn't wear un-Islamic clothing (necklace and rings). Shoaib totally lost it. He smashed a wall and had to be pacified by two friends. This was after he had smashed a guitar. Dr Sarmast wanted to talk with Shoaib's parents, but his dad was in the army fighting the Afghan fight, an insurgency in the Panjshir Valley, and there was no possibility his mum would come on her own.

Anger. So much anger, always there. Kids, adults. Men, women. Stress, pessimism, frustration, impotence. I could never reconcile the contrast between Afghanistan's gracious music, manners and kindness and the brutality of its reactive behaviour. How could you be calm here? How could you not get angry in that world?

~

Milad, the junior piano teacher and conductor of the Afghan Youth Orchestra, took an English exam to qualify for a scholarship in the United States. He, along with the pianist Elham (Wickham), failed. They both spoke good English, but the intricacies of grammar had eluded them. Milad looked devastated. I tried to comfort him by talking about how he could take the test again, how he must keep trying. He smiled that courteous, heart-melting Afghan smile and lisped a few words of agreement. Elham didn't seem to care.

There was something for Milad to look forward to, though. He and Fayez, the violin teacher, had been invited to New York state to take part in a music festival. They had been before and returned to Kabul, so both were granted visas.

'Great, Milad! You can really practise your English there!'

'Yes, teacher. I will practise, then come back and try again.'

~

Baset, the best trumpeter in Afghanistan, caught the attention of the principal trumpeter of the Philadelphia Orchestra, David Bilger. They started to have weekly Skype lessons and Baset's playing rose to a new level, easily as good as any student his age anywhere in the world. He started to learn Alexander

Aritunian's Trumpet Concerto and played his orchestra solos like a real professional. Perhaps, just perhaps, Baset would find a way to study in the States. He set up a fundraising webpage and the director of the Philadelphia Orchestra donated $5000; only $30,000 to go. Perhaps someone from the Kabul Bank would help. They seemed to have at least a billion dollars somewhere.

∿

My bank account had finally been set up, and I had been paid. I could now buy a motorbike.

Wais was the man to ask. I gave him a budget (less than $1000 for an Iranian-made bike) and a loose set of requirements (wheels, handlebars), and he went off in his magical Wais way to strike a deal. He came back later the same day with a selection of photos. Not really knowing what I was choosing, I picked a red bike and he delivered it the next day, lying on its side in a truck. It was the type of bike the Afghan police used, with knobbly tyres, wide handlebars and 200cc of power. It would do nicely. Since the bike had to have a Mexican name, he was called the Spanish verb 'to ride'—Montar, or Montie for short. Wais rode him around our garden, with Nacho, Jennifer, Cami and I bleating and skipping out of the way. Wais drove us to school afterwards and began his stream of consciousness English/Dari.

'BBC LONDON! JOHN KEEREE! HILAREE CLINTONN! JENNIFER BOOMBORI! EMMA DEEWANA!'

After eyeing up a few attractive women on the way, whom he called lunchboxes, Wais moved into a calmer phase. He smoothed down his greasy comb-over and complained about how much work he had to do and how his son was ill. We all sympathised and Wais asked for a loan of $20. I never expected to be repaid; this was Wais' way of making up his dismal income and I admired him for it. It was baksheesh—gathering in the most entertaining, kindest way possible. I knew that in a crisis, Wais would be there for us. After the French Cultural Centre bombing, when Dr Sarmast had been so badly hurt, Wais had helped people leave the hall before gathering up Dr Sarmast and driving him to the hospital.

One day at school, after a nearby bombing, I went over to the gateman's hut to say hi to Wais. He was sitting at lunch, his pistol on the table next to the tomato salad and kebab.

Guns became such mundane things, like a bucket or a pan. In Kabul people needed certain things, and, simply, one of them was a gun. David, an ex-marine and journalist in Kabul, walked around with a semi-automatic pistol in a casual bag over his shoulder. Soldiers swung their Soviet-era Kalashnikovs across their backs like a violinist on their way to a concert. Chris, the Greek god ex-commando, shoved his pistol down the back of his jeans, leaving a bulge like a colostomy bag.

Chris was an excellent motorbike rider, and one day took his girlfriend, Alyssa, and me out off-road riding. It was possible to do off-road riding right in the middle of Kabul, as the roads were not all paved, but we went out of town towards Qargha Lake and found an area of fields and streams where I could put Montie and myself to the test. It was ridiculously good fun haring around a paddock, creating my own fear for once. We rode back into town joined by an Australian miner called Kevin.

Chris ran out of petrol. Alyssa, Kevin and I were a little ahead of him so had to double back. Chris was pushing his bike towards a market area; it was a hot day, so he had taken off his leather jacket and his gun was clearly in view, the grip sticking out from his belt. Alyssa asked a policeman where we could buy some petrol and we headed further into the market area. Just as we were reaching the roadside petrol stall, a man came over with the policeman. He pointed at Chris's gun.

'You cannot have that.'

'Oh, it's okay, I have a licence for it.'

'Where is your licence?'

'It's at home.'

'Then you must all come to the police station. This is illegal.'

Well, it may have been illegal, but it was also becoming fucking scary. We were in the middle of a market with what turned out to be a plain-clothed policeman telling us we were breaking the law, a crowd of young men quickly swarming around us. As Chris had already said, guns only make everything worse. The events leading up to Farkhunda's murder swam in my mind.

Keep calm. Smile.

I offered the policeman a cigarette.

'No, I do not smoke. You need to come with us.'

The plain-clothed policeman took his mobile and spoke rapidly to his superior. Chris began to sweat heavily. We waited by the side of the road for forty minutes as the crowds continued to gather, were shoved away by the police, then gathered again. It seemed only a matter of time before someone came with a suicide vest. Alyssa began to swear at the police, pointing out what enormous danger we were in. I pushed my fear down into my trousers, where there was no gun, and wondered what my mum would say.

Chris called his friend Aman. A young man, no more than twenty-eight, Aman already had four children and a serious amount of money. Aman had grown up in Pakistan, worked with US Special Forces, spoke English fluently and ran a media company. In other words, Aman was a good man to call in a crisis.

Chris passed his phone to the plain-clothed policeman. I watched the policeman's face, until now barely polite, change to an expression of subservience.

We could go. Chris was told to go home and deliver his licence the next day to the police station.

We couldn't leave quickly enough. We rode to the Mexican House, leaving behind a crowd of Afghans looking resentful and confused.

When we arrived home we cracked open the whisky bottle. Chris, sweating all the way through to his gun, sat chain-smoking.

'I fucking hate this. I hate it that I can't do anything else besides fucking security. I don't know anything except fucking fighting. I fucking hate guns.'

～

Security guards in Afghanistan can earn enormous amounts of money. For ex-soldiers it is a natural career progression and can set them up for life. It is a world of fly-in fly-out rotations, intense periods of working and a feeling of brotherliness, and also of being trapped.

There is a particular fashion that security guards follow. In more casual settings these enormously muscled men (and very occasionally women) wear cargo pants, straining at their squat-enlarged thighs, t-shirts pulled tight over pectoral muscles and bulletproof jackets.

More official events, however, require a little more style, a little more thought. The ANIM orchestra was invited to give a concert at the Swedish embassy. The students looked exquisite, the girls in multicoloured Afghan dress and the boys in payraan tumbaan and glorious waistcoats. As with so many things in Afghanistan, we had to wait to begin the concert. A deputy minister of something important had decided not to bother coming on time, so we lingered for nearly two hours under the mulberry trees. The students were wonderful, sitting quietly and talking, or practising. I stood around chatting with Atesh, who would be playing the piano, and encouraging Laila to speak to as many people as she could. She learnt the art of schmoozing. Or networking.

'It's so easy, Laila. Just ask people about themselves. It's everyone's favourite subject.'

I spotted a couple of Swedish security guards with modern-art weapons and decided to try to engage them in a bit of a chat. With them constantly looking around at the garden where all the diplomats in Kabul were gathered, they showed me how they were dressed. It turned out they had to go to a special tailor to have their formal jackets made with extra room for their Kevlar vests. And the buttons on their dress shirts were fake; underneath the button was a popper, so the shirt could be easily ripped open in case of injury. I did wonder why they needed poppers when men with biceps that huge would have been able to rip open a steel drum without too much bother.

Once again, nothing in Kabul was quite what it seemed.

Men, men, men. So many men. I was stuck inside my hijab, inside my female body, and my old friend gender dysphoria came to say hello after a long, long time.

The everyday stress of Kabul, plus the extreme activity of teaching and carrying around double basses and cellos and chasing after kids, meant that after a few months I had become very thin. Yoga every morning for an hour and a half kept me fit, but I had lost my appetite. It was a feeling of wanting to disappear from my female body. As I lost weight my hips shrunk and my breasts became so small I could almost forget I had them.

But I did have them. I'd had a hysterectomy when I was thirty-nine because of fibroids, so thankfully I didn't have periods anymore, but what remained was a body and perceived gender that I had always, in the deepest level of my conscious-ness, hated.

When I had worked on the radio there was a question I sometimes asked an interviewee: what would they most like to be asked? It confounded people so I gave up asking it, except of myself.

The question I most wanted to be asked was: 'Emma, are you male?'

I looked around at the men in Afghanistan and I experienced the greatest envy I have ever known. Envy of their bodies, their beards, their friendships, their apparent sureness of their place in the world. It felt like I was banging on a thick window, looking in at the world of maleness, utterly distraught at not being able to get in. I would be forever stuck outside, forever on the wrong side. I looked to women and I could see nothing in common with them, neither with Afghans nor Westerners.

I had felt this before, but convinced myself that being androgynous was okay, that in fact, in the world of feminism, I had a duty to search for new spaces to be a woman. Well, I tried, I really, really tried, for feminism's sake, but I had a great tsunami of self-hatred heading straight for me.

I smoked endless cigarettes; I drank and drank. I began to seriously worry about becoming an alcoholic, but kept drinking anyway. I ate just enough to have energy to teach.

When I realised I was transgender, it was a life-destroying moment. Because I knew from then on that I would never be happy until I did something about it. But to do something about it meant possibly losing everything.

This thought, from my time in Pakistan, kept stabbing through my mind: 'You will never be happy, Ayresie. You must do something now, before you spin into another depression.'

This internal conversation harangued me without end: 'No, I can't. How would I teach here? What would I do? What would my mum say?'

Every day the same thoughts, picking away at my brain. A vice screwing tighter and tighter. As dysphoria and despair colonised my mind, I became unfriendly, irritable and unkind. Jennifer and Cami both noticed and asked me if I was all right, but my earlier experiences with depression had taught me to lie—yes, I was just tired. At home I hid away in my room after school, watching *Hogan's Heroes* on YouTube (somehow comforting) and searching female-to-male transgender resources. Just what the Afghan security services made of my Google searches I would love to know.

I felt I was preparing for a desperately dangerous journey that I would never, ever return from, but which I had no choice but to undertake. A final odyssey.

I understood now. There was no other way.

It was party time. Cami was leaving for a trip to see his wife so Jennifer, Cami, Allegra, Shabheer and I shoved ourselves into Shabheer's Toyota Corolla to go out for dinner. Le Jardin, a fancy French restaurant popular with expats, had burgers, pasta, beer and whisky. Eating there cost more than a local teacher made in a fortnight.

Cami suddenly announced that he needed black socks. Shabheer stopped the car in the middle of one of the busiest junctions in the city (just metres from where Farkhunda had been murdered), leapt out, and was back thirty seconds later with brand-new black socks. Two pairs. Four foreigners were left in the middle of the road in an unlocked car, ripe for the kidnapping. We merely sat in the car and roared with laughter at the danger of it all.

We drove past cyclists with impossible loads of cartons and vegetables on their bikes. We stopped at traffic lights and a gang of tiny boys dragged themselves up from the kerb to swarm around our car, begging for anything. A policeman held the hands of three kids to guide them across the main road. Soldiers kissed each other and held hands at a checkpoint.

We ate, we got pissed, we celebrated Cami's trip with pure joy in our hearts. We all understood what it meant to leave Kabul, because we understood what it meant to stay.

∿

Amruddin the rockabilly bass player sat with me in my teaching room, Beethoven glaring down from the wall. Amruddin told me a little about his life: his dad was a shopkeeper and he had five siblings, some from a different mother. Amruddin had a peculiarly high-strained voice, and asked me what he could do about it. The concept of polyps was a little beyond his English and my Dari, so I told him I'd have to get back to him. We returned to music; every lesson he brought me a piece he had found on YouTube and we sat and listened to it together, side by side, as the traffic rushed past outside. The look of energy and satisfaction and pure pleasure on Amruddin's face as he discovered different types of music was utterly glorious. He had found a recording of Bach's 'Air on a G String', which he wanted to play for his recital at the end of the year. I downloaded the sheet music and we started to learn it.

Amruddin's sound had developed enormously over the last few months, and as we played a few scales all the noise from outside receded into another world. I gradually became aware of students and teachers rushing around outside in the corridor, so I poked my head out to see what was happening. Jennifer was standing there, her face white.

'Did you hear the bomb?'

'No! What bomb?'

Only in Kabul could you ask such a question. And only at ANIM could the sound of a bomb be hidden within the sound of a double bass.

'Parliament. There's been an attack. There's been, like, a massive bomb! I can't believe you didn't hear it!'

The end-of-class bell had rung and students were running, panicked, from room to room. Meena the baby cellist was sobbing, Hafizah comforting her. Parliament was only a few kilometres away as the crow flies and as I stood and listened I could hear rapid gunfire.

Dr Sarmast seared through the school, his moustache shaking with fervour.

'Ms Ayres! What are you doing? Go to your class!'

I had come from the magical world of Bach and stepped into a calamity. I ran down the hallway to the grade tens' theory class. They were all waiting, silent, scared. I looked outside the window and saw the soldiers with their guns running uselessly to and fro, their teapot discarded on the ground.

I asked the students how they were doing.

'We're scared, teacher,' a two-metre-tall boy, Shiraz, answered.

I looked around at them and I could see how terrified they were. Their eyes were fixed on me, a little glazed, their usually lively bodies frozen on their chairs. Scanning the room, I tried to think what we could do if there was an attack at the school. I saw the grand piano and wondered if it would do any good to hide under it. The front gate was right outside our window, but it was unlikely the Taliban would be so polite and predictable as to come through there. I decided that we would all escape through the windows and make a run for it.

How could I tell these kids they would be okay? Why would they believe me, in this world where young men step into a room and blow themselves up?

I was as scared as they were, but I was the teacher.

'We'll all be fine. What's the best way to take your mind off being hungry in Ramadan? Work. So that's what we're going to do.'

And that's what we did. We revised syncopation, chord inversions and ornaments. After half an hour the mood had calmed and I played them some Arvo Pärt. Their faces drifted off, safe now in music's fold.

Dr Sarmast came into the room and told the students to go to the buses. School was over.

~

The next day I expected the students to be, for want of a better expression, a little shell-shocked. Not at all. Samia the violinist was even a little hyperactive, dancing down the corridor. When emotions get jolted so far one way they can swing back violently in the other direction, and that is what happened. The students were manic the day after the bomb, impossible to teach. The only one to protest was Baset the trumpeter. He posted on his Facebook about how dangerous it was to come to school, so he was staying at home.

Baset was, of course, correct. He was the only one to point out the real state of the emperor's new clothes. We were *not* safe at school. Dr Sarmast gave the odd hint that plain-clothed policemen were looking out for us, but the reality was that at school we had a low wall with a bit of barbed wire. We had a few lacklustre soldiers. We had no fire plan, let alone an evacuation plan. Jennifer, Cami and I gathered and discussed what we could do. There were exits at the end of each corridor, but they were locked. Jennifer climbed into my cello case to see how many children we might be able to hide in there. We decided the only way was to climb out of the windows and run for the gates.

That plan was scuppered a few days later. We arrived at school and turbaned workmen, acting quickly for once in Afghanistan, had fastened thick steel bars onto all the downstairs windows. We were now in a prison of music.

8

Minds of children, hearts of ancients

It was a rare thing to see a foreigner out on the streets, especially in the west of town.

'Look, Wais! A foreigner!' I pointed out as Wais drove frenetically through the back streets to the Mexican House, taking a different route every day.

'No! Foreigner, no. He is Afghan. Just he has been eating a lot of burgers.'

The ethnic mix of Afghans means that you can see nearly every skin colour, hair shade and tint of eye in humanity and still everyone is Afghan. Blonde hair and green eyes like Nazira, pale brown hair and green eyes like Atesh, auburn hair and freckled skin like Farhad, dark hair and olive skin like Shaperai, dark hair and pale skin like Hafizah. Jennifer was fortunate in being able to blend in; with her beautiful Japanese and Swedish heritage, she looked completely Hazara. Although this did beg the question whether it was safer to be seen as a foreigner or a Hazara, especially when she was riding her motorbike around Kabul. Cami, with his dark skin and green eyes, also looked Afghan, but Allegra and I just couldn't quite pass. For Allegra, perhaps it was her face shape and tall, thin body; for me, my pinker skin, height and muscularity.

I was desperate to make my way through Kabul as a local. I was desperate to do something other than school, home, school, home, very occasionally a motorbike ride. I also badly needed more Islam-approved clothes. Luckily for me, in Afghanistan there are invisibility cloaks called abayas, voluminous black capes that draw around the neck and go all the way to the ground. One Friday Shabheer took Allegra and me shopping in his Corolla and we dressed in huge black abayas and hijabs, only our blue eyes and rosy faces showing.

'Walk behind me, and don't look anyone in the eyes,' advised Shabheer.

At a local shopping centre we followed my fake and Allegra's actual husband around the tiny stalls, like a mini harem. Every stall had naked mannequins and minimal dresses, which women wore at home, and no one gave the mannequins or us a second look. I thought of the diplomats trapped in their embassies, safe yet almost completely secluded, and I knew where I would rather be. Every shop assistant I spoke to complained about how bad the economy was and how they wanted to leave. If everyone left who said they wanted to, very soon Kabul would be empty.

Shabheer had lived in Kabul his whole life. He had been born at home, his mother giving birth to twins completely on her own. Shabheer and his twin brother, Shaheer, were children during the Taliban rule of Afghanistan, and they had been two of the first students at ANIM. As we drove around the city of his birth he talked about growing up in the civil war. At junior school he learnt to count with the Taliban method: one bullet plus one bullet equals two bullets. Two guns plus two guns equals four guns. His teachers hit the students, made them hit each other, held them upside down and hit them, threw glass cups at them until the cups and the students were smashed. Some of those teachers were still at ANIM. Shabheer's family had stayed during the civil war, his mum a doctor, his father a bank clerk. Such safe jobs, such perilous times.

Shabheer was utterly pragmatic about the problems with his country. His face looked resigned as he said how everything Afghans did was with aggression: they bred dogs only for fighting; they fought in their cars, at work, with their families, when they went to the market; they fought other ethnicities; they fought the land, the weather, invaders.

Both he and Wais were clear and pessimistic; they said there would never be peace.

Allegra was looking tired. She and I had a running joke of belittling each other's instruments, the oboe versus the viola (my old instrument).

'So, Allegra, when are you going to give up playing the oboe?'

'Well, Emma, I don't know how you even managed to get your viola into the country. I mean, they must be illegal, right?'

It was a brutal type of teasing that never failed to make us laugh, but Allegra had stopped playing along with me for a few days.

She sat in the office with Sama and Parwana, filling in visa applications for a trip to Germany that some of the students and staff were taking. Sama's office was always calm because it was a refuge from students, but local teachers came and went, always with a chat and smile for Sama and Parwana, a curt nod for me. It seemed I had not been forgiven for trying to help them with their ear training and music theory teaching. The most I had got from them in recent weeks was the Islamic teacher telling me I looked like a man. Not exactly news to me.

'Allegra, what's up? Are you okay?'

Allegra's work was never finished. She often stayed at school long after us Mexicans went home, writing Dr Sarmast's emails, arranging music, doing endless re-editing of proposals, writing speeches and creating PowerPoint presentations for Dr Sarmast when he travelled to easier places—New York, Hong Kong, Beijing—to accept awards or speak at conferences.

'Shabheer and I are going to leave.'

Allegra had been at ANIM for nearly five years; of course she would leave at some point, but a little bit of me had thought she and Shabheer would stay forever. Then I remembered. There is no forever, especially not in Afghanistan.

Allegra had started the process of applying for a US visa for Shabheer.

'It is the hardest, most complicated thing I have ever done, applying for this visa.'

For Allegra and Shabheer, as always in Afghanistan, it was now simply a matter of waiting.

～

News reports grew more and more horrific as the wave of refugees from Syria, Iran, Iraq and Afghanistan skyrocketed. Every day there were pictures of bodies on beaches, in the sea. A queue of humanity walked towards Germany, and now, in that queue, was a trumpeter with the body of a gymnast.

Shaheer—brother of Shabheer, junior teacher and assistant housekeeper to us Mexicans—had given up completely. He often failed to come to school, and when he was there he gossiped and sulked. At home he had given up as well, lying in his little house smoking, drinking whisky.

And one day he was gone.

He hadn't come to school, but since that wasn't unusual none of us thought anything of it. When we went home, Shaheer wasn't there. At dinner he wasn't there. We looked in his room, but nothing, just cigarette butts.

Allegra called. She told Jennifer that Shaheer had gone during the night, first to Herat in the west of Afghanistan, then on with a people smuggler to Iran.

When Sama, one of the secret yoga ladies, found out, she said simply, 'If everyone leaves, how will the country get better?'

Shaheer said goodbye to no one, not even his twin brother.

～

Laila had started to use vibrato regularly (when you shake your hand to make the note more beautiful) and was exploring higher regions of the viola. She stood tall in her lessons and danced through Dvorak's Humoresques; she was learning to love each note. Laila was a joy to teach because she was curious, but I had also discovered just how fragile she could be. A fragility beyond the usual teenage turbulence. When there was a problem in her life (other than living in a war zone, keeping the school she attended a secret, being beaten by her uncle) I could see her face turn inwards again and an anger burn up through her eyes. I would always try to help, but there were so many things that were irreparably fucked. Sometimes Laila said things that made my heart stop with joy, but on these tumultuous days it might also shudder with horror.

The orchestra had a TV recording playing 'Women's Song', the composition by Ustad Shefta. It was a gruelling couple of days in the studio and we played the piece twenty-seven times one day (Jennifer, Cami and I had a bet and I won) and twenty the next, in true boot-camp style. Dr Sarmast said after these two days that finally the sound of the bomb at the French Cultural Centre had gone from his head. The problem for Laila was that the song was going to be broadcast around the whole country and she didn't want her family to see her, as they still didn't know she was at music school. She decided she couldn't risk it and didn't play. It was awful for her. She wept in my room the next day, but she wasn't crying for herself.

'Teacher Emma, I am crying for all the women and girls in my country who want to play music but can't!'

I will never forget the dignity of this young woman, standing with her beloved viola in her hand, tears falling down her steep cheekbones, her shoulders heaving with a fathomless sorrow.

We eventually talked about lighter things, and she asked me for ideas for gifts for Afghan Mother's Day.

'What about cooking your mum a meal? Or making her a picture? Or writing her a letter?'

'But, Miss Emma, my mother, she cannot read.'

Laila and Nazira were good friends; they quite often came into my room if they had a free period and helped me teach the babies. Every student had two lessons a week, as well as a group lesson for their instrument. In Hashi's lesson one day he was having trouble keeping his left elbow up and also sitting up straight. Stocky little Hashi, always a tad bewildered by the world. Laila and Nazira could see the seriousness of the situation and decided to help. The two teenage girls surrounded the pre-pubescent boy, one holding up his arm, the other with her hand on his back to keep him straight. Hashi was left wide-eyed in the middle, trying not very successfully to play the cello. His dirty feet curled under the chair, as if to escape the persecution. Laila suggested I build a medieval-style pulley system of chains to hold various instrumentalists in the correct position, but I preferred Laila and Nazira.

Jennifer had started baby quartets as well and we both wrote and arranged music for their standard. Watching the babies grow as musicians was like watching a time-lapse series of photographs; they were growing almost implausibly quickly. Late one Thursday afternoon, after school had finished, the four cleverest and most gifted of the baby group came into my room.

'Teacher Emma!' said Aman, a violinist. 'We have a name for our quartet! The Babur Quartet. Do you like it?' (Babur was the first Mughal king and buried in Kabul.)

'I *love* it, Aman. Now, what's happening?'

'We want to stay after school and practise quartet, but nobody will let us.'

They stood there together, musicians to their ten-year-old cores. Aman, a pale-haired, almost corn-coloured boy, utterly brilliant. He had learnt in his five months with Jennifer what most kids would take two years to learn. Always quiet, studious, a little apart from the group. And Hamed, son of Massouma the tea lady: handsome, cheeky, wildly talented and worryingly lazy. Shahed the viola player, cocky, surly, funny and running swiftly towards puberty. And Meena, darling Meena. The baby Jacqueline du Pré of Kabul.

'Teacher Emma, we want to play!'

I went to ask the principal, but they had to go home. It was the end of a long, dangerous week and they needed to play at other things.

When I came back and told them, they looked furious, as only a person can who has been denied what they truly love.

∼

Children, especially those who have so much stress in their lives, need endless reassurance in their learning. Fatima had plateaued with her progress and she was beginning to lose happiness in her playing, so I started a new game called 'Tiny Teachers'. I sat with my cello, everything in the wrong place. My back was slumped, my feet were crossed, my cello was too low, my elbows drooped and my wrists were bent in.

'Fatima, tell me, what am I doing wrong?'

'Everything, teacher!'

Fatima grabbed the offending part of the cello, or arm, or foot, and put it into the correct position. As soon as one part improved, I put another bit in the wrong place. It became a giggling game and ended with Fatima shouting 'Teacher!' and giving up. She fake-frowned and started to play Suzuki's 'Perpetual Motion', this time with everything (almost) in its proper place.

Fatima was fast approaching puberty. She scowled into her lesson one afternoon, her hair plaited and a frown on her face. In recent weeks she had developed a particularly dark sense of humour, and when I asked her where Meena was she said, 'Dead, teacher. Taliban. Suicide bomb.'

Just at that moment Meena popped her head around the door and collected her cello. Fatima looked sideways at me. She had finally cheered up.

～

A pattern emerged over the months at ANIM. There were periods of calm, almost predictability, and then something truly terrible would happen. It was as if everyone got a bit bored.

I had noticed over a week or so that Mohammad, the charming guitarist, had not been at school. Considering the number of people leaving the country, I assumed he had also gone and didn't even bother to check.

This wasn't the case. Mohammad had killed a man.

Allegra told me over our lunch of greasy Kabuli pilau.

'I've been here a long time and heard some terrible things, but this story is the worst.'

The story, within the confines of truth in Afghanistan, was this. Mohammad's brother's wife had run off with another man to Europe. This was the worst thing that could happen in any Afghan man's life. It was a shaming of the most deplorable kind and, in a world of gossip, impossible to hide from neighbours and friends. Mohammad had come to his brother's aid as he confronted the family of his wife. At some point the family had said something so terrible that Mohammad had no choice, according to his world, but to show how strong he and his brother really were. He stabbed one of the men, and killed him.

And then Mohammad came back to school. I had never knowingly met a murderer before, and to be honest I felt extremely uncomfortable. This thin, deeply polite man standing in front of me had taken a knife and plunged it so hard and deep into another human's body that he had died. I just didn't have the emotional vocabulary to deal with it. Why would I? Why should anyone?

Allegra told me more over the next few days. Mohammad had bribed the police by selling everything he owned—his car, his business, his office. There was a rumour of US$10,000.

With this bribe he had bought his freedom. The family of the murdered man was refusing to drop the charges, though, so there was still doubt whether spending even this amount of money would mean he could stay out of jail.

When I tentatively asked Mohammad about it he shrugged his shoulders and said calmly, 'Everything will be all right, teacher. In Afghanistan, you either kill or die. It is as God wills.'

Fucking God.

Mohammad came to my room a few weeks later, his guitar in hand.

'Teacher Emma, can you listen to my music?'

I sat on the floor as Mohammad took his guitar onto his knee and, with exquisite delicacy, caressed it. The weak, late summer sun teetered through the window behind him and the saddest, most winsome music trickled into the air.

'I wrote this music in jail, teacher. And I kept it in the jail of my head.'

Minds of children, hearts of ancients. It was phrase I couldn't let go of, turning it around and around in my head. I thought of Mohammad, who had murdered a man for disrespecting his brother, of Hafizah, who ignored me if I criticised her playing, of the war lords, who refused to negotiate with each other and make better lives for their people, of Wais, who carried a gun and sent pictures of kittens to Allegra on Facebook, of the ANIM teachers who shunned me because I had merely tried to help them expand their teaching. Offence was taken so quickly to guard ancient honour, and petulance prohibited any other act than revenge.

~

It was Friday. We needed to do something normal.

'Guys, let's go out. Let's put nice clothes on and go out for dinner.'

We called a taxi and went to a restaurant called Table Talk, close to the city centre. Table Talk was favoured by NGO workers and rich Afghans, but its security was not tight enough to allow diplomats or UN people. There was a garden with covered wooden platforms where you could eat, drink tea or smoke a water pipe or hookah. And they served an excellent beef stroganoff.

As we were tucking into stroganoff, Mexican chicken and pizza, we started to hear distant gunfire.

No problem, it's a wedding, I thought. Weddings were carte blanche for firing endless rounds into the sky, and dozens of people died every year from the falling bullets. The gunfire continued and seemed to get more intense, coming now from all directions.

'Um, should we be worried about those gunshots?' we asked the waiter.

'I can't hear anything. Don't worry, we have a gun behind the coffee machine. You'll be safe.'

So we decided to kick back and order a hookah. Why waste energy being scared? Assessing how much danger I was in was a daily process. We started to smoke the hookah, the water bubbling in the bottom, but the gunfire seemed to get louder. Shit. Should we go get the waiter with the gun behind the coffee machine? Should we run?

Just one more puff on the hookah . . . and more rapid gunfire.

I still believe it was a mistake anyone could make. The rapid fire of an AK-47 sounds exactly like delicious mint and apple smoke being gently sucked through water and that's all I have to say about the matter.

∾

Nacho—otherwise known as Nachissimo or the Great Kebab— had lice. The poor kid was so itchy-scratchy we had to wash him with a special shampoo. Jennifer tied him to the apple tree and hosed him down as he bleated and butted his teenage horns against my thigh. He had a few other things to be annoyed about: his taste for roses and laundry meant nowhere was safe for Shersha to dry our clothes, so we asked Shersha to put up a low fence between the house and the garden. Nacho watched dubiously with his horizontally slitted pupils as the fence went up, then he came over to me for reassurance and a bite of my trousers. Just like my own, Nacho's world was gradually getting smaller. No more sticking his head through the kitchen window in the morning for a head scratch. No more wet hijabs for a light snack.

Still, Nacho remained quite the socialiser. When we arrived home, he would gambol over and hang out, trying to eat my cigarettes. One morning he ate all the coffee grounds that had been thrown around the headless, leafless roses. All he needed was whisky for a trifecta of addictions.

One lazy Friday afternoon he blew himself off again, then headed over to me for an after-sex fag.

Ah, Nacho.

∾

Sometimes it felt that the most interesting things at school happened after the lessons were over. Atesh and Laila would stop by for a chat, children would come and watch cartoons with me, we had skipping competitions and juggling practice, Jennifer would show me hilarious cat videos on Facebook and give me chocolate, boys would romp in and tell me about flying their kites with razors on the strings to cut their opponents down or they'd invite me for a game of cricket, Cami would come and improvise on the cello, Wais would fling his enormous bulk in and sing and pluck the double bass, older girls would do their make-up and take infinite pictures of themselves on my phone. It was young Afghan life and it was simply and utterly glorious.

One day Parwana and Sama came down to my room after school, playful smiles on their faces. Finally, secret yoga could restart. I put a large whiteboard in front of the window, they took off their hijabs and plastic shoes and we did sun salutes and warrior poses. They loved it. They loved the invigoration of their bodies after a day at a desk and a life of repression. They had both grown up under the Taliban and studied at secret schools, so secret yoga was nothing new.

Sama had been extremely polite and reserved when I first moved to Kabul, but over these now six months I had learnt what a powerful, witty and moral person she was.

And, as it turned out, an excellent actor.

Samir the violinist had a problem: he was wonderfully absent-minded, as good musicians often are, and kept leaving his violin in practice rooms at the end of the day instead of returning it to Koko Abdul. Yo-Yo Ma once left his cello in the back of a taxi, Lynn Harrell did too, and I once left my viola at a motorway service station—but I'm guessing we all learnt from this and it was both the first and last time we ever did it. Not so for Samir.

He needed to be taught a lesson.

I went up to Sama's office one morning to escape the kids and do some uninterrupted work. Sama had a huge grin on her face and a violin case on her lap.

'What's going on, Sama?'

'Hello, Emma Jan.' (Jan is an affectionate addition to a name, much like dear.) 'Samir left his violin out again yesterday so I am teaching him a lesson.'

A few minutes later Samir came up the stairs looking extremely worried, with Koko Abdul close behind him, his broken bow at the ready.

'Sama, er, has anyone seen my violin? I think I might have left it out last night . . .'

'Samir, really? Again? No, I haven't seen your violin.' (By now his violin was hidden under Sama's desk.) 'Go and look for it. Properly.'

Samir slumped off and Sama went in a flash from terrifying teacher into hysterics as she mimicked the look on Samir's face.

A few minutes later Ustad Bakhtiari, the man in charge of computers and the CCTV cameras, came up to the office.

'Ustad, can you do me a favour?'

Sama explained the whole thing and the trap was set.

Samir returned, violinless.

'Samir, Ustad Bakhtiari here says there was an intruder last night in the school. He is going to look through the tapes and see if the intruder stole your violin.'

All the time this proper, smart, good Muslim woman had a look of the greatest severity on her face. It was all I could do to not explode with laughter.

After what must have seemed like days to poor Samir, Sama called him back up to the office to say that the violin had been found. Samir was banned from using it for a week and given a beginner violin to play instead. Sama spent the rest of the day laughing, and Samir spent the rest of the day running from broken-bow-wielding Koko Abdul. He didn't forget his violin again.

∾

The Afghan Women's Orchestra had grown even more with the arrival of the baby string players: cellists Meena and Fatima, viola player Marzia, and violinist Suweta. The rehearsal room was definitely too small now, so Allegra negotiated with Ustad Shefta to swap rooms with the boys' band. Shefta refused at first, but after a comparison of how many students there were in each ensemble, the girls easily won. It was possibly the only girls' victory in the history of the country.

We settled into our new room and the babies were officially welcomed into the ensemble. I sat in rehearsal with Meena and Fatima as we played an arrangement by Allegra of Amy Beach's Waltz. The girls had been invited to play at the World Economic Forum in Davos, Switzerland, the following January, so they needed to prepare a program.

Allegra was brilliant at creating arrangements that catered to each individual player in the ensemble. Medina was an exceptional oboe player, so she was given the melody much of the time. Bibi Mina on trumpet was also a strong player, with a Chet Baker-style crack in her sound. She played with a sadness that caught your heart, so she was often given more melancholy tunes. Laila became quite frustrated as she was awarded 'only' accompanying parts.

'Teacher Emma, why should I always play these simple notes? Why do I not get the tune?'

'Laila, welcome to the world of the viola player. If you were playing in the Berlin Philharmonic Orchestra you wouldn't have the tune either.'

She was clearly not satisfied with this answer, so Allegra changed Laila's part to match her ego.

One of the hardest things in orchestra is not the notes you have to play but the rests when you don't play. If you look at any orchestra in the world, going through nearly every player's head (yes, even the viola players) is the following: 1-2-3-4, 1-2-3-4, 1-2-3-4, 1-2-and-3-4, 1-and-2-3-and-4, and so on, ad infinitum.

This counting becomes such second nature that eventually it slips down into a deep recess of the brain while you consciously think about other things: musicality, sound, do I fancy the conductor, shit, I haven't done my taxes. But it takes a while to get to that happy (or unhappy, in the case of taxes) place, and every musician has to go through the process of learning to count consciously. This is tough for any young person, but in Afghanistan it became a minute-by-minute struggle with each student. I never quite worked out why this was so, but one theory I had was that, because of the enormous pressures all the students lived under, having to think about things like everyday survival, the fact of whether they came in a little bit early with their F-sharp crotchet was perhaps not top of the list of priorities. I did know that when the students counted, and when they played perfectly together, a different feeling reigned in the rehearsal room—one of calm, happiness, team pride.

One student who did count was baby Meena, who had grown a lot over the last few months and had lost her baby cheeks. Her thick plait fell beyond her waist as she sat with her cello, furiously counting for the Waltz. I sat beside her, playing along or pointing at the music when there was some doubt. I watched as she mouthed her counting in Dari and played her part: 'Yak, doo, say, yak, doo, say, yak, doo, say.' Sol rest rest, sol rest rest, re rest rest, re rest rest.

Allegra had written a pizzicato part, mostly open strings, so that Meena and Fatima could learn how to play in orchestra without having to worry too much about hard technical music. It was perfect pedagogy. Meena occasionally looked up at me, smiling with glee at finally being here, playing with the big girls.

The Afghan Youth Orchestra rehearsals were not going so well. Students rolled their eyes as we played an arrangement of 'Ode to Joy', Nazira sat playing her Bach instead of Beethoven, the percussionists went back to their tardy ways and the whole group sweated and stank its way into musical pointlessness. They charged through every piece as if the sooner they finished it, the sooner they could get to lunch. And their minds were being colonised by the news of so many people leaving. I wondered if anyone wanted to be in Afghanistan, let alone at ANIM. I had loved playing with the orchestra just a few months ago, but now there was a bitterness to their playing that deeply disturbed me. There was also no feeling of being *inside* the music.

There is a musical term, a direction sometimes written by the composer at the beginning of a piece, called 'pesante'. Pesante literally means heavy and ponderous, but it's not just that. It is a feeling of making each note last as long as possible within the pulse of the piece, of enjoying each moment for what it is. A good example might be Elgar's 'Nimrod' variation, or Brahms's Symphony No. 1.

No matter how hard Cami tried conducting the orchestra— and he was an exceptional conductor—he simply could not get the players to slow down. Everything was rushed. In the end he resorted to a brutal method: he asked Oman, one of the older percussionists, to keep a steady, slow beat on a drum. We played along to it, punched into slowness. Afterwards Medina the oboist played a virtuosic, intensely fast scale, as if the feeling of pesante was a bacteria she needed to wash off.

The problem with the orchestra was we didn't have anything specific to rehearse for, and these young musicians simply adored performing. They also didn't have anywhere to play. In the past the orchestra had performed at the French Cultural Centre, but that had been blown up. ANIM had been given money to build its own concert hall, but this had turned into an Afghan morality tale.

The building had begun in 2013, to great fanfare and hope that Zubin Mehta might even come to conduct the orchestra. By 2016 the hall was still not complete. The structural work had been done, but then the company in charge went bankrupt. New tenders had to be submitted by other companies to finish the work and this next step was eternally delayed. Now the building was suspended in time, a mere prologue of a performance space, the walls bare concrete and an empty stage waiting. Waiting. Everything in Kabul either raced ahead without stopping, like the music, or never got going at all. The ANIM concert hall was caught in a barbed-wire web of corruption, bureaucracy, laziness and politics. The same web that held the whole country in its grasp.

Security had become so bad that an audience of diplomats and high government officials would not come to any venue outside of the green zone. Well, if they wouldn't come to us, we would invite people who could come. Jennifer and Allegra started to organise a concert to be held at ANIM for parents and Afghans without a security detail. And if the concert hall were still a mere shell we would have it in a tent.

~

Atesh came into my room after school one day, baby Meena in tow with her cello.

'Teacher Emma, do you have the piano part for Meena's pieces? We are going to play together.'

Atesh had made massive advances on the cello without really doing any practice (he truly didn't have time). He was such a natural musician that he simply wanted to know everything, so he spent a huge amount of time practising the piano, having conducting lessons with Cami, and composing and arranging his own music.

Atesh had also caught on to the fact that baby Meena was extremely talented. Her talent illuminated her and Atesh was naturally drawn to an equally gifted musician. Meena was approaching the end of the first Suzuki book after only six months. She constantly asked for harder and harder scales and worked out for herself how to play a three-octave C-major scale, high up on the cello's A string. I wouldn't usually have encouraged this, but Afghanistan was a special situation. Just as the occasional chaos at the school was training the students for life outside, Meena needed to learn from an early age how to work things out for herself. There wouldn't always be a cello teacher at ANIM.

'Yes, of course, Atesh. Here you are.'

I handed him the piano part and they walked off together, the cleverest people in the school.

I went down to their practice room a while later to see how they were getting on. Meena could play all her pieces from memory and she sat looking at Atesh as they played 'Long, Long Ago'. It is a mournful little tune that allows a student to embrace a soulful feeling of playing. Atesh added a few jazz chords as Meena sang on her cello. Atesh improvised with harmony like a puppy, as if chords were a football. As they played I imagined a time before the Taliban, before the Coalition intervention, before corruption and despair, when these two could have lived safely.

Atesh came to me the next day to show me a photograph. During the summer break he had visited a cousin in Nuristan province. This is a place where foreigners—even Afghan foreigners—regularly get killed, so Atesh had carried a Kalashnikov with him.

There is an archetypal photograph of a Taliban member. You probably know the one I mean: pakol on his head, gun over his shoulder, fierce mountains in the distance. Atesh showed me his photograph. He was standing with mountains as his backdrop, a pakol on his head, a Kalashnikov over his shoulder. And Bach running through his veins.

∼

A massive, massive truck bomb went off in a very crowded, poor neighbourhood, which happened to also have an Afghan Army base. Over a hundred people were killed immediately, many more terribly injured from glass. The blood banks were empty. Amazingly only one kid from our school was injured. Jennifer received a text the next day from an Afghan doctor friend of hers saying they urgently needed AB-negative blood. I insisted on going straight away to the hospital; that's my blood type and the most rare. As we were working out how to get to the hospital in what was now a virtually locked-down city, Jennifer received another text. It was too late.

My brain emptied, shredded apart by the sheer horror of what I hadn't done. If only I had thought, like so many thousands of Kabulis had, to go straight to donate blood, maybe things would have been different. A person might still be alive. Something broke in me in that moment. My perception of the world took a bitter, violent twist. Something in my emotions hardened also, only because, if it hadn't, I would have left Kabul the next day. And this enormous determination came and sat right in the middle of my heart. I would not fuck up like that again. I think it was at that moment that I realised where and how I would be living for the foreseeable future. I couldn't let myself cry, as I was at school and I knew that if I started it would be a long time before I stopped. I went to teach and came home to drink. There was a lot of whisky drunk over the next few weeks.

Islam prescribes very swift funerals; over the following days funerals were all I could see, all I could hear.

The next night, Cami and Jennifer went to the British Embassy Ball, an annual event to raise money for Afghan charities. They looked gorgeous, Jennifer in a little black dress with vertiginous heels, Cami in an Afghan-made tuxedo. Cami really went for it with the dancing and split his tuxedo trousers right down the crotch in a dramatic Colombian move. Thank heavens he was wearing black undies.

I spent the evening watching *Better Call Saul* and was outside having a fag when I heard another bomb. Close, perfectly sonorous. The thing about the sound of a bomb is not so much the sound itself, but the silence after it, as if the sound is really a gathering of all the sound around, put together in one perfect instant. It's the opposite of a beginner musician's sound— that begins with scratchiness, but is ultimately full of life. A bomb is a gorgeous sound, but it ends everything. This time it was the police academy. Over twenty young men were murdered as they returned from their weekend off. And the British continued to dance.

The kids were no different the next day from any other. There was no choice; feelings *had* to turn from terror to laughter. Hysterical laughter, laughter that I found I grabbed onto and rode as long as I could, because I knew I'd need that feeling later that week, that day, that hour.

I needed music more than ever. To play it myself, to teach it, but also to simply listen to it. I became obsessed with Beethoven and his logical phrasing, a counterweight to what my life had become. I began to go down to Cami's room after school to sit with him; Cami was always exquisitely calm. We sat together, imprisoned by a marimba and bongos, and listened to Beethoven's *Coriolan Overture*. The terror of the first chords could never match the terror we were living through, but they somehow made sense of it. We listened to the searing horns, the strings running for their lives, the timpani firing shots into the sky. Cami, and Beethoven, brought me back to safety.

～

We three Mexicans were siting outside only a day or so later, listening to Arvo Pärt mixed in with the call to prayer from the local mosque (a surprisingly pleasing mash-up). Jennifer answered a call from Allegra. As the call went on, Jennifer looked increasingly horrified.

Four suicide bombers with suicide vests had just been arrested in the compound next to the school. We sat, incapable of anything. Over the next two hours, more and more news came. They had been taken for 'questioning'. Two more had escaped. The principal wanted to cancel school the next day, but the police said to carry on as normal. We planned our defence of the kids and how we would escape, packed grab bags, and somehow all slept.

Every morning I got up to do yoga and meditate. This was not a day to miss that. As I came out of my meditation, I felt so scared. There was no question I would miss school, so I lay on my yoga mat and tried to brainwash myself into being brave. Save the kids. Look after others. Have courage. Think of yourself last.

Where does terror go? I couldn't work out what to do with this new feeling. I tried putting it in the sensible part of my brain and that functioned quite well—work stuff out, be practical, think logically. Then that part got exhausted and I tried stuffing this monster into my humour part.

What's the similarity between a suicide bomber and a viola solo? You know they're both coming, but there's absolutely nothing you can do about it.

Then, like a hot coal that has to be passed from hand to hand as quickly as possible, I threw the monster to my spiritual side: we all die, this will be quick. But, just as we fool ourselves into thinking our hands aren't being burned by the hot coal because it only spends a little time in each hand, still, that time builds up and up, and in the end your hands are burnt beyond repair. That was how it felt. The monster might not be here in my consciousness, but I was aware it had dug far down into my deep subconsciousness and now I was searching for it, because I didn't like it being in there and I didn't know what it was going to do.

My classroom that day overlooked the front gate. I found myself checking the gate every few minutes, watching who was arriving, wondering what was inside the big truck that had just pulled in, wondering whether the armed police would turn and shoot *us*, not *them*. And then, slowly, something extraordinary happened. I was teaching beginner cello and I cared more about the sound Fatima was making, the shape of her bow hold, than whether we were all about to be blown up. Those calloused hands, this young Afghan girl, she was playing such a simple tune. A scale in D major, sometimes going up, sometimes down.

Fa fa sol la la sol fa mi.

Re re mi fa fa-a mi mi.

So simple; so profound. The most famous tune in the world: 'Ode to Joy'.

At the end of the day Koko Abdul, the instrument caretaker, came to my room. He was doing the vacuuming, dressed in his child's ski suit. Vacuuming in Kabul was the very definition of a Sisyphean task and I always admired Abdul's optimism that some day the dust would stop. He turned off the vacuum, pulled out a long object from his back pocket and I braced myself for a lashing. Not that I had done anything wrong, but that didn't always matter with Koko Abdul.

It was his flute. He hopped up onto a chair and played an Afghan folk melody, his feet swinging in dead sandals.

An Afghan hell; an Afghan heaven.

9

A hologram of belief

A small note if a mullah happens to be reading this: Guys, when you're doing the call to prayer, can you sort out your microphone technique? It's a microphone. That means you don't need to shout.

And banging it before you start—we can hear that.

Also, can you get Bose or a quality company to sponsor you? Your sound is always so shrill. You guys need bigger bottoms.

∽

Milad and Fayez, the junior piano and violin teachers, had gone to upstate New York to play in a festival. They had travelled twice before to the States and had returned, so they had been granted visas. Elham, the Wickham-esque pianist, had visited the States as well, but he had a visa to stay longer and a chance to get into college without passing his English exam. Being granted a visa was no sure thing at all. I had heard a story of an Afghan who had worked for an

American media company in Afghanistan for nearly twenty years who had been refused a tourist visa.

The gossip at school became about one thing only: whether Milad and Fayez would return. At school each day the students stood around whispering, like members of the French royal court before the revolution. There was a hideous feeling of doom.

I couldn't stand it. Whenever I saw people standing around just chatting, I asked them what they were doing to improve their lives.

'Nothing, teacher.'

'Exactly. Please go to your room and practise.'

They would slump off, only to be seen in the next period doing the same thing, over and over.

We teachers were really no better. In our breaks all we could talk about was what decision Milad and Fayez would make. They both had many opportunities if they returned. Milad conducted the orchestra, made excellent arrangements, played the piano beautifully and only had to improve his English to be able to take up a scholarship in the States legally. Fayez played many gigs outside school and was adored by his students; Jennifer was working on a scholarship to a college in Indonesia for him.

Milad and Fayez had hope, but they also had deep responsibilities to ANIM and to their families; Fayez, for instance, was the sole provider for his family. Milad and Fayez were due to come home via Istanbul, on the same flight as Sama and some students who had been playing in Turkey. The days eked on, those two weeks covered by a veil of morose, worried waiting.

~

After the hell of the truck bomb and the suicide bombers, we Mexicans decided we seriously needed something to cheer us up. Our despondency was beyond the curative powers of any alcohol.

We began to talk about getting a dog. There was an animal shelter in Kabul called Nowzad, founded by a British Royal Marine who wanted to provide care and shelter for cats, horses and dogs particularly. It is common in Muslim countries for dogs to be ill-treated, and Afghanistan was no exception. Packs of bloody, mange-ridden dogs scrounged food from rubbish tips, the humans around them showing their hatred with the rocks they threw at them. Shabheer and Shaheer were angelic exceptions—they had both rescued animals from the side of the road and brought them to Nowzad, and Shabheer and Allegra had two rescue kittens.

'Let's go to Nowzad and see what dogs they have.'

It was agreed that I would eventually bring the dog back to Australia. Easy.

We rode our motorbikes over to Nowzad that Friday, past parliament where the bomb had gone off so recently. We asked the policemen outside the way, and for directions were offered tea and talk of Afghanistan's emerging cricket team. As for a dogs' home, they had no idea. We decided to follow the sound of the barks and were finally let through thick blast-door gates into the home. The dogs were better protected at Nowzad than we musicians were at ANIM.

We were shown around by one of the Afghan vets and fell in love with at least five dogs. And eight cats. Oh, and a donkey.

An English vet called Louise was in charge. When I asked her about eventually bringing the chosen dog back to Australia, she simply said, 'Not a chance. First of all, it will cost you US$20,000. Then the dog has to be in quarantine in Dubai for six months. And, after all that, there is no assurance the dog will get into Australia. We have only ever managed to get one dog through.'

So, that was that.

We were going to have to look elsewhere for happiness.

Jennifer had been keeping in contact with Shaheer via Facebook as he sometimes walked, sometimes took a truck further and further from Afghanistan, closer and closer to Germany. Before he left I had given Shaheer my old iPhone 4. I now considered the weirdness of this whole thing: a refugee, now illegally in Iran, yet somehow buying phone credit to keep in touch via Facebook.

There was no news from Shaheer for more than a fortnight, then he messaged Jennifer from Turkey. A gang had attacked him and the other people travelling with his smuggler and three refugees had been murdered. Shaheer only survived by climbing a tree. That little, lithe gymnast's body had saved him, but the gang had stolen his passport, his money and his phone.

The group had tried six times to get beyond Turkey, once being arrested and shot at in Bulgaria, but were still stuck in

Istanbul, now desperate. The hope of his journey had gone; the thrill of travelling to his future has been shoved aside by trying to survive the police, the weather, the Mediterranean and a greedy smuggler. Shaheer had twice got on a boat to go to Greece, but each time the flimsy plastic vessel had sunk, sometimes with as many as ninety people on board. They were made to board by men with guns, then rescued by water police and left to try again. Winter was coming there as well, so how would he survive?

Shaheer was officially and mentally stateless. He could not go forward; he would not allow himself to go home. His twin brother now had a constant look of sadness on his face. Shaheer's story was whispered around the school, as a deterrent to some, as a mere fable to others who believed they would do better.

The stories of the departed became like a hologram of belief. Horror, like Shaheer's story, from one angle; hope, like Milad and Fayez's, from another; and finally, envy—an ANIM driver had taken his whole family to Germany for US$75,000 and had gained permanent asylum.

~

As Shaheer's grim story unfolded, the day finally came for the return of Milad and Fayez. Jennifer had been in contact with Fayez via Facebook and was optimistic that morning; I heard her singing show tunes as she got ready upstairs. There was no hint that Milad and Fayez were even thinking of staying in the US.

The Turkish Airlines plane landed early in the morning and Sama arrived at school by 9 a.m.

Massouma the tea lady called me up to Dr Sarmast's office. I left Meena to practise her Bach and ran upstairs.

Dr Sarmast's office was always a place of calm and order in the school. A place to hold optimistic meetings for the happy future of music. Not today. As I walked in, Jennifer was in one of the armchairs weeping, a box of tissues in front of her. Dr Sarmast sat beside her, his head bowed. As he looked up at me, I knew immediately what had happened.

Milad and Fayez had not returned.

We all sat in silence. I ventured that maybe they would still come, maybe they had missed their flight, maybe they had decided to stay for a few days, maybe they would realise their mistake and return. Maybe. Maybe.

I looked at Dr Sarmast, his full, strong face, his thick moustache, usually so powerful. This had defiled him. His face was impassive, but his eyes and mouth tightened as the country of his birth took another bite of faith from him. It had aged him in a minute and he looked nothing other than defeated. Of the five junior staff from the beginning of the year there were now only two left: Masjedi the percussionist, and Sameem the tabla player.

'This is a very frustrating time.' And Dr Sarmast asked us to return to work. He stayed in his room, alone.

～

The news spread through school, as if the rules of time didn't exist. As if the knowledge had always been there, only allowed to be spoken of on that day. Fayez's students wept as they

talked. Little Cevinch, Samia, Sombal, they had all treated
Fayez like their big brother.

And Milad. He was the natural student leader of the school,
on his way to being the best composer and pianist in the
country. What were all the students meant to think when
these two crucial people chose the US over them, their musical
family? It was a devastation depicted only in tears.

I feel that Jennifer never really recovered from this loss. It
was hard not to see it as a betrayal. She had given up so much
to teach in Afghanistan—she had resigned as director of her
Suzuki school in Hong Kong, a comfortable and ordered life,
and devoted endless hours to coach Fayez in how to teach, how
to live, and how to be grateful for what he had, both then and
for the future. We all wept in some way on that terrible day.

As the school carried on, we had to pick up the pieces of
Milad and Fayez's duties and responsibilities. Cami took on
conducting the orchestra full time, including making new
arrangements of pieces with Allegra. This, on top of his own
percussion teaching, was a huge workload. Jennifer and I now
had no assistant for the strings studio and we all had to pick
up various theory and ear-training lessons with the babies.

I couldn't help but feel angry towards these young men.
They had left behind people who needed them. They had let
down Dr Sarmast. They had threatened the chances of other
students being granted visas. They had smashed a hole in the
new musical building that was being made, brick by arduous
brick. Is this what every student would decide, once they got

to eighteen? Was this all the school was doing—providing a way to escape?

The true ruin of what these young men had done was not shown until a few days later. As I walked up the stairs to the library, Shahed looking gleeful because I had asked him to carry my viola, I saw a woman in a hijab sobbing as she walked down the stairs. It was Fayez's mother. Dr Sarmast had just told her that her son would probably never come back. Fayez had not said goodbye.

~

After the three junior staff left, many people thought the school would implode and we would be left lost, ashamed even that we had let these three go. But the school seemed to thrive more than ever before. We took all the best players from each department and made a chamber orchestra, conducted by Cami, playing arrangements of Afghan and Western music for two concerts, one at the Australian embassy, another at the US embassy. We had a TV recording and a concert for Save the Children, with a specially composed anthem for children that would be sung all around the country. Things that began at ANIM now reverberated throughout Afghanistan. The only things remaining of Milad and Fayez were the paintings they did on the new safe-room door. Would they be forgotten? Or would these Afghans meet up in decades to come and talk of these times? And would they be thankful for the decision they made?

Who, eventually, would be left to remember?

But there was such hope left behind. It felt clearer somehow: the people who remained were either too young to know anything different or still had some yearning to stay in their country.

~

Throughout this time Atesh had been away. I was very worried, as all I could glean was that he was ill in Pakistan. Then good news, of a sort: he had chickenpox and had gone to Pakistan to recover. He came back after three weeks, thinner, scarred, his green eyes less lively, but his presence around the school still as calming and vital as ever. Of all my students, he was the one I loved the most.

When I talked to Atesh about Milad and Fayez leaving, he didn't hide his disappointment. As he saw it, they had a duty to serve their people, and they had made a huge mistake. Just like Laila, Atesh saw the beauty of his country so clearly: the land, the people, the traditions, the music. At that point, Atesh had Cami to teach him conducting, Allegra to teach him theory and piano, and me to teach a wild ride of pretty much anything, so Atesh was happy to stay. But what would happen when we all left?

Atesh believed he had good things to say through his music and surely that could help. But how? What difference can music make to anyone if a whole family has been wiped out by a drone bomb? Atesh said that he would sometimes lose hope and think about behaving like the junior staff and many of the students—just hang out, have fun, laugh, look at Facebook. But, through his music, he believed he could raise a voice of peace and freedom and equal rights; by composing songs, he could show what was right, not only to Afghans but the whole world. Atesh wanted to use his music as a weapon, to fight for peace. It struck me at that moment how like Dr Sarmast he was.

Atesh, more than anyone I met in Afghanistan, had a profound sense of social justice. He walked everywhere, all over town, to the rich and poor parts, and he saw so much injustice. He had lived in an orphanage with the poorest of people and had lived apart from his parents during his most important infant years.

'I consider it my duty to help my people.'

'But, Atesh, why do some people here hate music so much?'

'Maybe they have seen so much music used in bad ways. Like the music for the dancing boys [young boys dressed in women's clothes and made to dance for older men]. But in the days of the Prophet there was music and it was allowed.'

'And, when you play music, is it a world you don't want to leave?'

'Sometimes I think we shouldn't even have this world we live in. But then I think, no, we can make this a better place.'

'In your dream world, what will happen in your life?'

'I think that by the time I'm very old Afghanistan still won't be how I want it to be. But I have hope that for the generations after me, if there is a good foundation for them, we will one day hopefully have a better Afghanistan. I'm not sure I want to go abroad to study. If I can't find teachers, or if the school closes down, I will try to study abroad, to see what the world is like, how other students study, other teachers teach.

'I have such passion for music. Other things I'm no good at. I'm not physically strong, but I can help most with music.'

A few days after his return Atesh came into my room, his face flushed with a profound experience. He had been walking to school through an area where there are hundreds of drug addicts and street kids, close to where Chris had run out of petrol. The addicts squatted on the ground under a bridge and in the middle of a four-lane road, smoking heroin underneath their shawls. They looked like a Christo project, with scarves instead of white sheets. As he walked, Atesh was listening to Bach's 'Air on a G String'.

'Teacher Emma, it all made sense! Listening to this music, seeing these poor, dirty children and the addicts, and listening to this beautiful music, it was like seeing everything in slow motion. I could see so much pain. It all came together as one.' Atesh had seen what music meant. It meant everything.

During all this time of gossip and abandonment, Laila remained quiet. One day she came to her lesson and seemed uncharacteristically vague and disinterested, so I decided to be a bit tough on her, thinking that would get her over a lazy patch. How wrong I was.

As I was lecturing her on doing better practice, Laila started to cry. She turned away from me.

'I will never be able to be a musician in Afghanistan. I must go to Pakistan. And I will never be able to play my viola again.'

She said that her family might leave at any time. She wouldn't be able to say goodbye. There was nothing we at school could do except try to persuade her mother not to let her go and to withdraw Laila's engagement to a family friend.

The terror in Afghanistan was everywhere, but least of all because of the bombs. The terror lay in not knowing who would be there at school the next day and what their family had made them do.

Imagine having to give up your favourite thing, the thing you love beyond measure, the thing that has kept your life together for years. Imagine having to say goodbye to all your friends and going to live in a strange city, confined to four walls, having baby after baby. This was what Laila was facing. She wept, she sobbed, she let tears fall down her face and all I could do was imagine the same and how yes, I too would weep tears to cry a lifetime away.

Nobody could live through times like these and not be forced into a fundamental shift in their thinking; for me, the ligament that tempered my reason was severed. After eventually finding out that those suicide bombers had indeed been targeting the school, it didn't seem centrally dangerous to me anymore. Instead I released myself into emotions that veered wildly from side to side and I delighted in the smallest of things, the simplest of gestures, the kindness of my family of music. Jennifer, Cami, Allegra and I formed a bond of musical soldiers that we all knew would never be broken, wherever we were.

I would have died saving them, and they would have done the same for me.

Those few weeks were strangely exhilarating, simply because I found an increasingly deeper love for music and for teaching. I found resilience, humour, practicality, lightness and immense anger within myself. I let go of any preciousness about how life should be and instead accepted what it handed me.

'Some moments are more precious than long periods in our lives. But how do we wrap our hearts around them?' mused Jennifer.

One incident perfectly illustrated this unfettered time.

Marjan, the violinist with the thieving brother, was learning a tricky student concerto. At the end of the piece was a series of chords with three, sometimes four notes, and Marjan was making her way through it with Jennifer in the last lesson at school. I could hear from my room that much fun was being had across the corridor, so I went and joined Hafizah, Samia and Nazira as they all cheered for Marjan, egging her on to her next chord and her next tiny achievement. Finally, after much struggle, she got to the end and we all went wild with clapping and whooping. We were happy, simply *so* happy that Marjan had made it.

She had made it to the end.

～

I walked with Baset, the brilliant trumpeter, down the corridor to a chamber orchestra rehearsal after school.

'Teacher Emma, I have good news. I have been accepted at Interlochen high school for the Arts in Michigan.'

'Oh my gosh, Baset, that is the best news I think I have ever heard. Congratulations!'

Baset glowed with pride. He was trying to get to the States legally and this was an enormous step. All he needed now was a little more money from his crowdfunding page, and a visa. The all-important visa. The visa that now, after Milad and Fayez, would be so much harder to get.

True to Afghan type, just when things seemed to be stabilising there was a massive earthquake. A literal earthquake.

The orchestra had gone to a TV studio to record the audio for the 'Afghanistan Children's Anthem'. It was written by Ustad Shefta in a classically Soviet-realism-meets-five-beats-in-a-bar style. Ustad Shefta was himself a curious mix; many times I saw him play the fool hilariously, then take on a different mantel as an elegant, virtuosic clarinettist. He had returned to Kabul after years overseas and his students adored him.

Shefta had a unique history of writing anthems. During the mujahideen time he had written a national anthem for Afghanistan for choir and orchestra; this had been used again as the anthem during Hamid Karzai's time, until Babrak Wassa, an Afghan–German, composed a new one. (This anthem is really worth listening to—strident, swashbuckling, switching from major to minor within a single phrase. And ending, I hope not prophetically, in the minor.) In the intervening Taliban era,

Shefta's anthem was forbidden and the Taliban summoned him to write a new one for choir alone.

Shefta said this would be very difficult, but he didn't actually say no at the time. He went home and told his family about the meeting; they knew that if he didn't compose the anthem he would be executed. They all knew what Shefta had to do—run away immediately. By the next morning he was ready to leave. He didn't have much money so he could only go to Pakistan, but to earn a living he needed to bring his clarinets.

This was the sticking point. Every border crossing had checkpoints where the Taliban would check for forbidden items such as playing cards and instruments, so it was going to be extremely difficult to take his clarinets out of Afghanistan. Shefta had heard about a guitarist leaving the country who had taken the fret board and the body of the guitar apart, removed the strings, and then used the fret board as a walking stick, claiming he was lame.

How could Shefta get his clarinets out of Afghanistan?

First of all, ditch the case. He wrapped the separate parts of the clarinets in his clothes, put them in the bottom of his suitcase and piled more clothes on top of them. He then put a chessboard on top of everything. Shefta used the biggest one he could find so the Taliban couldn't miss it: chessboards were also forbidden but the punishment for having a board game was not as severe, compared to the death sentence for having a musical instrument. His hope was that putting the chessboard at the top of the suitcase would distract the Taliban at the checkpoint.

Shefta took the bus to Pakistan, travelling with a relative who was completely unaware of what Shefta had with him. They arrived at the border, the Taliban controlling the checkpoint. Shefta got off the bus with the suitcase and a Taliban soldier came up to him.

'Open the suitcase.'

He opened it; on top was the chessboard.

'What is that?! Don't you know that is forbidden?'

Shefta feigned ignorance and said he hadn't heard about the banning of board games.

'Come with me to see the commandant.'

He took the chessboard, closed the suitcase and gave it to his relative, who crossed over the border. Shefta said this was the scariest moment of his life; he wasn't sure if he or his relative were going to live through it. The commandant questioned him and he continued his pretence.

'From today I know it is forbidden—I will break it myself!'

Shefta threw the chessboard on the floor and it smashed.

This is how Shefta got his clarinets into Pakistan. Once there, he worked as a wedding musician, the same job he had been doing in Afghanistan. The problem was, he still had to return to Kabul every month or so to bring money to his wife and two boys. He would put on his worst clothes and pretend he was a homeless man to keep a low profile; in Kabul he was a well-known musician and he was worried someone would spot him and hand him over to the Taliban.

Shefta lived this life of weddings, exile and disguise for nearly three years, ending up in Islamabad. He never got used to the hot climate, though, and began to dream of somewhere colder. Many of his relatives had moved to Bishkek in Kyrgyzstan (very cold, lots of consonants), so he went to stay with them for a few months before moving to his aunt's flat in Moscow. Shefta lived in Moscow for ten years, again earning a living as a wedding musician with the same clarinets he had smuggled under the noses of the Taliban.

In 2009 Dr Sarmast called Shefta and asked if he would like to teach at ANIM. They had been schoolmates years before; Dr Sarmast was in the year below Shefta at the original School for Fine Arts, along with the sergeant major teacher Ustad Nader. These Afghan musicians had all taken a long path back to Kabul.

The recording of the children's anthem came on one of the last warm days of autumn. All the students were in a good mood, sticking their heads out of the school-bus windows on the way up the hill to the TV station. They were happy for a break from the routine of their life. And hey, lunch would be better.

The engineers took about three hours to set up the microphones; after lunch we were finally ready to record. I made a quick nip to the loo before the recording and while I was taking a piss in a wooden shack with no foundational structure at all, one of the biggest earthquakes to strike the Hindu Kush in decades hit. And I didn't notice a single thing. Seriously. So when I walked back to the only slightly less flimsy TV studio and saw all the students running out of it, I immediately thought, Oh shit, there's been an attack. But the kids were laughing. What would make them run and laugh at the same time? I walked in further; only then could I see the boom mikes swinging and the studio lights swaying from side to side. I decided at that point it was probably a good idea for me to be outside as well.

The Pakistanis measured this earthquake that I had weed my way through at 8.1 on the Richter scale. It killed about four hundred people, including twelve schoolgirls who were crushed by schoolmates as they escaped a building. Once again, Afghanistan had given us all a ferocious reminder: this land would never be calm. And this time, the reminder came from its very bedrock. Afghanistan's fate was literally written in stone.

Chris and Alyssa, the Übermensch couple, came round for dinner. Shersha had made my favourite meal of cumin- and saffron-spiced meatballs, affectionately dubbed Shersha Balls. He had also made a trifle; that still seems funny to me. Anyway, Chris and Alyssa needed our help.

They were animal mad and at that point had a small horse, two goats and five dogs. The dogs and the horse lived with them in their house close to the middle of town. It was a scenario I found hard to imagine, until I visited one Friday for pizza and saw all the dogs and the horse happily trotting around in a large garden. There was one dog, though, who was outside the pack. This was the one they needed help with. Chris and Alyssa knew we had been thinking of getting a dog, so they asked us if we could take her for just a few months.

They returned the next evening in their green Land Rover Defender, Chris with his gun still stuffed in his jeans, and the dog stuffed in the back. She ran out, sniffed around the garden, ran away from Nacho and rolled over on her back to be tickled. So that was that. We named her Pancha, 'calm' in Spanish. She looked like a small German shepherd, with a grey tint to her coat. She was gentle, strong and independent. After tummy tickles she went off and lolled by the wall, watching us with her brown eyes. I had the feeling we would do just nicely for her.

Pancha settled in with us impeccably. She slept on her cushion in my room; every morning we got up together and she showed me how to do the downward-facing dog yoga pose properly. Pancha barked at Nacho then ignored him. Sometimes all the Mexicans would run around the garden together, Nacho bucking and rearing on his hind legs, Pancha panting, Jennifer throwing her head back with glee, Cami giggling like a young boy. Pancha came and sat on the cushions with us in the evening, somehow aware of her role in calming us. Pancha was perfect.

∽

The day came for our school concert. Except for embassy and presidential palace performances, it had been a long time since the school had had its own concert. A suicide bomber had ended the last truly public event so this was a magical, vital day. Virtually every student played or sang in one of the orchestras, chamber ensembles, wind ensembles, baby string ensemble or girls' ensemble. The concert was partially funded by the German organisation GIZ as part of their Playing for Change Day. Allegra had sent the music for the 'Women's Song' to various schools all around the world and had made a video that combined flautists in the US, guitarists in Germany and ANIM students. It was truly beautiful to see these young school students sharing in a piece of Afghan music written by a man who had fooled the Taliban.

A huge tent was erected in the dusty playground and gradually parents and visitors came to sit down. The babies were beside themselves with excitement and I had the hilarious job of wrangling them before our performance. This wasn't just herding cats—it was herding Afghan kittens. We made our way onto the stage and played 'Twinkle, Twinkle, Little Star' in four-part harmony and a piece I had written called 'Race to the Stars'. The babies were brilliant. Rohullah, the lonely viola player, stared out at the audience, beaming with confidence. Meena had put special beads in her hair and even Hashi had put shoes on especially for the event.

The Afghan Youth Orchestra came on stage and played 'Russian Sailor's Dance' by Glinka, and Beethoven's 'Ode to Joy' with tabla introduction. Over forty young Afghans on stage, all playing precisely, joyfully together, with Cami our very own Gustavo Dudamel. The parents, mostly mothers, sat in the audience, their hijabs tilted a little back so they could hear better. Smaller siblings perched on their knees or ran amongst the roses. After the concert the mothers kissed their children, hugged them, and thanked us teachers. In all the times I had spoken with the students' parents, this was the only occasion when they had no stress on their faces. For these last few hours we had all forgotten where we were and how music had to so often be hidden. We had sat together in a rose garden, under a tent, with few guns in sight, simply enjoying the music. The policemen on guard stood at the back, their guns for once by their sides, hands free to clap.

This was a special day. A day to always remember.

~

If something as desperate as gender dysphoria and profound self-hatred is destroying your mind, there's nothing like a few suicide bombers to distract you. That's what happened over those few weeks. I had reached the point of realising I had to do something about the disaster inside my head but, hey, that could be conveniently ignored when there were mass killings to think about instead.

But at some point, even in Kabul, calm eventually came, and with it the return of my inner misery. Perhaps this was why there was so rarely calm there. It gave you time to think.

It was Eid al-Qurban, the festival honouring Ibrahim's willingness to sacrifice his son for God, and I decided to go to Istanbul for a few days. I needed space to consider what the fuck I was going to do.

Us Mexicans, meanwhile, had to make another hard decision: what to do with Nacho.

The dear goat was growing into a fine fellow. This meant his headbutting had become more determined and painful, his eating even more prodigious and his blowing himself off even more frequent. Allegra (I'll blame it on her) talked about the luxury of keeping a goat as a pet when so many people in the city, let alone the country, didn't have enough to eat. Perhaps this Eid, the festival when a goat is traditionally slaughtered, was the right time to give Nacho to Shersha. He in turn would have the animal slaughtered, and would be able to share the meat amongst his family and friends.

It was a dismal decision, but there was really only one choice. We asked Shersha if he would like Nacho and he bowed, thanked us, and took the goat away as he had arrived all those months ago, in the boot of his 1986 Toyota Corolla taxi with dollar signs on the door. Jennifer wept. Cami and I were more sanguine about it, but each of us understood the difference Nacho would make for dozens of people. Shersha had spent a lot of time with Nacho and I had often seen him tickling him under the chin, or feeding him leaves from the grapevine, so it was no surprise when he said it had been hard to have Nacho slaughtered. Still, there was no room in Afghanistan for sentimentality. Shersha said Nacho had given them forty kilos of meat. And that was what we really wanted.

I said goodbye to Pancha (who was perhaps wondering if it was safe to stick around after Nacho) and headed off to Istanbul. Even though I had been out of the country just a couple of months earlier, somehow time in Kabul moved so strangely that it felt like years since I had been in the Western world. Even stepping onto the plane crossed a boundary of smells, safety, expectation.

I had booked a little hotel in the backstreets close to Taksim Square. This was my first trip to Istanbul so I felt somehow obliged to go and see the tourist places—Hagia Sophia mosque, Topkapi Palace, the Roman cisterns. But I just couldn't. A huge, crushing wave of depression fell on me, taking every atom and dragging me down, down, further than I had ever been before. I knew what was happening and I was terrified. Perhaps more terrified this time, because I knew where my mind would go. I had only had a few months to recover since my last horrific journey, and my scars were still raised and weak.

Despite the massive things that had happened to me over the last few months in Kabul (suicide attacks, fleeing students, more bombs), there was only one thing I could think about—transition.

I lay on my hotel bed and spent day after day searching female-to-male (FTM) websites, looking for some clue about how to start. I was searching online for bravery. I watched video after video of transgender men on testosterone, men who had had chest surgery to remove their breasts, videos of one-, three-, six-, twelve-month updates. I looked into the Internet for my own future and I saw hope, frustration, misery, happiness and infinite courage. Courage I knew I had to summon for myself.

I at least knew where to start. I emailed Adrienne, the therapist from my depression in Sydney, and asked if I could talk to her about this. She wrote back immediately and said yes. We would have a session on Skype and see where we went.

I cried a lot during this time. No, not a lot. A sea. An ocean. Fucking endless tears. I felt intensely alone and, to use one of the simplest words, sad. Sad at what this would do to my life, my family, my relationships, my own body and, of course, my work. To transition in Kabul at ANIM would be too much to ask. What would happen after that? How could I expect to carry on teaching? Who would want to go out with a mutilated person who would no longer physically be either gender? And I felt a great shame. I think that was the worst, really. The shame of the unwilling lie. Imagine yourself being forcibly disguised as another person for decades. And, because that is how you have had to grow up, because that is how people accept you, you have had to remain that way. But you know, you *know*, in the most solid way possible, that it is not the real you. That inside, screaming, is the true, suffocated you, and that you will go mad if the outside of you does not match the inside. I was tired of lying to myself, and to others. So staying female-bodied was clearly impossible, yet my only choice was to end up with the body of a mythical creature. It was an acceptance of the greatest magnitude.

After I had written to Adrienne I felt my depression lighten a little. I forced myself to go sightseeing and, on the streets of Istanbul, trod the path I had come to know so well: being seen as a man in one place, a woman in the next. I realised that the world I was so scared of was one I was already living in. And at least with hormone therapy and chest surgery I would be able to love a little more of myself than I did then.

You won't need much tweaking

Winter was coming. The swallows had gone, Shaheer's and their house now completely empty. The air was slowly becoming brown with the smoke of wood fires; the mountains were disappearing from view and we wouldn't see them again from the city until spring. Due to the pollution and worsening security, each day limited our view of the beyond. The sounds of the city changed—the ice-cream carts with their perpetual 'Happy Birthday to You' theme replaced by the potato man, the onion man, and sellers of cauliflower and the emperor of all fruit, the pomegranate. Drinking fresh pomegranate juice, glimpsing the Hindu Kush, with the smell of wood and kebabs all around—those moments became my blessing.

I returned to Kabul feeling raw and exhausted. Those five days in Istanbul had scrubbed me clean but left me vulnerable. I knew I couldn't keep this enormous thing from my Kabul family, the Mexicans, so that Friday I gathered Jennifer and Cami into the kitchen and told them.

They sat and listened. They watched my lips tremble as I told them how long this had been with me and what it had done to me. And then they hugged me. They both simply said, 'We love you. What can we do to help?'

And they called me their brother.

After this enormous release, going back to school felt like a breeze. It was even more of a breeze because about forty of the students had suddenly left for Turkmenistan. The president of Turkmenistan had been at one of the school performances at the presidential palace, and was so taken with the students that he had invited them to play in the capital, Ashgabat. They had a week's notice to prepare. At school, only the younger students and a few older ones were still around, so it was an unexpected bliss for ten days. Jennifer and I revised the string curriculum, I restrung the double basses and checked the cellos, and we started to plan for exams at the end of the year.

The students returned from Turkmenistan sunburnt and thrilled at their holiday treat. Dr Sarmast returned furious with their behaviour. It seemed the girls and boys had been openly cavorting, complaining about the food and showing general disrespect to their hosts.

One thing that constantly made me curious was how these students learnt how to behave in the world. Many of them came from such large families that individual moral guidance was virtually impossible. Others had no parents present at all; they were either so distant they could give no parenting to speak of, or they were dead. I thought of my own upbringing and how my mother had drilled me in caring for others, behaving with consideration for the larger group, not being selfish and, yes, how to eat politely. But there were also deeper moral lessons, many of which I had learnt from books such as *I Am David*, *Swallows and Amazons*, *The Lion, the Witch and the Wardrobe* and *The Tale of Two Cities*. Books about how to be the best person you could, how to be brave, how to be kind. In Kabul I never saw children reading any books apart from their schoolbooks, even those kids who came from wealthier homes. No time, no money, no mental space. Of course. They would glean moral guidance from their Koranic studies, but the pressures of everyday life meant that it was almost impossible to not be, to put it simply, selfish. There was always a crisis to worry about or gossip over; how could you look into yourself and your own behaviour in such a place?

Dr Sarmast said the school had to do something about this. I couldn't have agreed more. We decided to have a series of talks in January, during the winter academy that was run through the school break, in which the students would learn about discipline, table manners, behaving politely amongst strangers and personal hygiene. So hard, in a place where tampons were virtually impossible to find and showers were often restricted due to cost and availability of water. How much could things improve?

∾

As winter drew in, Shersha suggested we have a kebab party in the garden, us Mexicans, Allegra and Shabheer, Shersha and his three boys, and our new assistant housekeeper, Shazadah. Shazadah had worked for Allegra and Shabheer when they first got married and Shersha had asked him to come and work for us. He had grown up in a tiny village on the road to Jalalabad and was the local boy made good. The villagers called him the film-star boy, because he worked with foreigners. Where Shaheer had been morose and unmotivated, Shazadah worked cheerfully and enthusiastically. His one problem was that he was quite deaf. As one of his main jobs was to answer the doorbell, he missed a lot of work opportunities.

Shersha marinated what seemed to be most of a goat, made another trifle, put rugs and cushions out in the garden, bought Coke and orangeade and brought his three boys over in his taxi. Shazadah and Shabheer lit the coals for the barbeque and we gathered shawls and lay under the stars, eating this simple, perfect food. The boys, Bilal the oldest at about thirteen, stood apart from us, nervous of these foreigners and their dog. Pancha prowled around the edge, staring with her brown eyes at the nearest human until they couldn't bear it any longer and threw her a piece of meat.

BOOM!

A bomb went off, by the sound of it only a few kilometres away. Bilal immediately burst into tears and ran over to his father, whimpering. Shersha took him into his arms as the younger boys looked on, not sure what to do. It was a sound I had become so used to that I had forgotten how terrifying it actually was, especially for a child. I went over to Bilal as well, to try to add to Shersha's comforting, but this only made things worse. Bilal could only stand and shake, frozen to the spot. We quickly packed up the food and rugs. The party was over, the trifle uneaten.

∾

Security continued to get worse as the political squabbling carried on between Ashraf Ghani and Abdullah Abdullah. The economy was failing due to corruption and low investment, and millions of young men had no jobs, no hope, no way to support their families. Signing up to the Taliban, or now the better-paid ISIS, became an economic necessity. Against these new fighters, the poorly paid Afghan Army suffered enormous casualties, leading to more squabbling, less confidence in investment, and the cycle of violence continued. My stress levels clearly rose too as I started to feel phantom earthquakes. Airport attacks, guesthouse bombs, parliament, ministries, embassies, kidnappings and, in October 2015, the fall of Kunduz to the Taliban. One day Jennifer and I walked around the perimeter of ANIM, trying to think like a terrorist making an attack against the school. Even with our innocent musician brains we spotted many places where people could come into the compound: a low wall here, a mere jump onto a building and down there, even a ladder left conveniently by a high wall.

We went to Dr Sarmast. Our feeling was that, even if we couldn't have the level of protection of the secure zone, there were still many things that could be improved. A blast-proof gate had been installed but was often left open. There were gun turrets, but they were usually empty, with the policemen more interested in tea than safety. As for any type of plan in case of attack, there was none. We had asked Dr Sarmast about taking the students through the steps of evacuation as a drill, but he said it would scare them too much. We had security cameras and a security officer, but he seemed to spend most of his time asleep in his blacked-out room. We couldn't escape through our now barred windows and the exit doors were locked. We had a panic room, but it was on the first floor, with windows. We wouldn't stand a chance.

'We will have a security meeting.'

Dr Sarmast instructed the security officer, Aziz, to make a detailed plan and instruct us the following day. Aziz had been working at the school for three months by this point. He looked shocked, as if this was entirely outside his job description. He tried to gain more time, but Dr Sarmast was adamant.

The next day after school we all gathered in the upstairs rehearsal room. All the teachers, except Dr Sarmast, were there, foreign and Afghan. Beyond music, our safety was the one thing that united us.

Aziz stood at the front and drew a rough map of the compound. He then proceeded to outline a security plan that I think everyone there, and the students too, could have done a better job of. In the event of an attack, Aziz told us, we would stay in our rooms until Aziz came and knocked on our doors and told us to either go to the panic room or leave the building. I pointed out that any terrorist worth their bullets would seek out the security officer and kill him first. And what was the point of waiting in our rooms? To practise our scales? And how would we leave the building with only one way out?

Aziz's ideas for the separate practice building were even worse: he suggested the students there should climb a ladder to the roof. At this point the Afghan teachers rose up as one and said how ridiculous it was to expect terrified children to climb a flimsy ladder to an uncertain future. If we'd had any rotten tomatoes they would have been chucked at Aziz mercilessly. He left the room, I hope ashamed at how he had let us all down.

Jennifer reported on the meeting to Dr Sarmast the next day and suggested we ask her boyfriend, Alex, to make a plan instead. Alex had worked in Afghanistan for several years and knew a great deal about security. True to his nature, Alex made the most wonderfully comprehensive plan—but it was so detailed that we mere musicians couldn't quite take it in. We were all grateful, but what we really needed was something in the middle. It never came from Aziz, who prevaricated and stayed sleeping in his room when Dr Sarmast was away. The sad truth was that, for the rest of my time at ANIM, we stayed safe by chance.

Every day I saw the tragedy and problems of Afghanistan demonstrated at ANIM, the macro in the micro. It only made me more pessimistic about the country's future. Aziz clearly not truly caring about the safety of the students or the teachers. Most of the students gossiping about the future, rather than actually doing something to shape their own. The Afghan teachers' suspicion of us foreigners. The deep frustration of Dr Sarmast, a Westernised Afghan, about his own people. The inability to plan for anything because of government bureaucracy, greed and corruption.

Inshallah. Always inshallah.

This phrase—God willing—was the downfall of Afghanistan. Because God expected us to work harder than that.

Winter continued its descent, the cold dribbling on my skin. No matter how many clothes I wore, I simply couldn't get warm. I had lost so much weight that all my natural insulation had gone. Emotionally and now physically, I was defenceless.

On 11 November 2015, thousands of Afghans, mostly Hazaras, marched through the streets of Kabul demanding justice. Seven Hazaras had been murdered a few days earlier in the southern province of Zabul. The victims—four men, two women and a nine-year-old girl—had been abducted and had their throats slit. The marchers carried their coffins through the city, women breaking with tradition, as in Farkhunda's funeral, by carrying the women's coffins.

The march came from the west, past the drug addicts of Dehbori, towards the university and directly past ANIM. Only a maroon plastered wall separated us from potentially one of the most violent events of the year.

The first thing I noticed was the sound. I was teaching young Sultan, an outrageously talented tabla player who had picked up the double bass in a flash. As usual in his lessons,

I played him a piece, he played it straight back to me, and we moved onto something harder. Still a young teenager, Sultan liked to move around a lot in his lessons, so I had him expend his energy on skipping for a few minutes. As he practised double jumps and one-footed hops, from the distance I became aware of a sound I had never heard before.

It was the sound of death marching. It was the sound of death protesting. A silent noise, almost a suppression of sound, and then the chanting, the shouting, the wailing, the rage.

All Sultan's ebullience was soaked up into the vortex of that sound. He looked at me, boy dimples crushed, his face overtaken with stress.

'What is that, teacher?'

'I don't know, Sultan. I'll go and check. Stay here.'

I went into the corridor, where students were standing in groups, hushed. Jennifer beckoned me to come upstairs to the library. There below us on the street were thousands and thousands of people. And in the middle of them, held aloft like grim trophies, seven coffins, one of them unbearably small.

The marchers were demonstrating against the lack of security in the country and President Ghani's lack of care for the Hazaras. Every single person in the country could have demonstrated about the same issues, but things were particularly tragic for these people. They, amongst all the ethnic groups, suffered the largest losses at the hands of the Taliban and ISIS. What had been happening to the Hazaras over a very long time had a name. It was genocide.

Hafizah stood with Jennifer and me. She watched the protestors and turned to me, clearly very scared.

'Go downstairs, Hafizah. Go to my room and we'll have a lesson.'

The sound of the march lessened a little as I went downstairs. By now Hafizah, Nazira and Aziza, a pianist and double-bass player, had joined Sultan.

'Teacher Emma, do you have this in your country? Do you have these marches?'

'Yes, for sure, but about different things.'

When the students had been so scared after the parliament bombings we had done some intense work to keep their minds off what was happening. I used this hour while the march went past to tell them about the demonstrations against the Iraq War, and the civil rights marches in the States in the sixties. They learnt about Martin Luther King, segregated schooling, slavery, institutional racism. They were surprised to hear that so many people in the States were not allowed to vote until relatively recently. It seemed to make them feel a little better about their own country.

Winter brought cold and with it domestic danger. Most people used wood-burning stoves to keep warm, and one day Hashi came to his lesson with his right hand bandaged. The stove, or bukhari, had fallen on his hand, crushing and burning it.

Then, an even worse accident.

Hamed, the youngest child of Massouma the tea lady, hadn't come to school for a few days and neither had his mum. Finally the other babies reported what had happened.

Massouma had been cooking on a stove attached to a gas bottle. To keep the house as warm as possible, she had taken the stove into the living area. The bottle had exploded, seriously injuring both Massouma and Hamed. They were away for weeks. When they returned, the skin on their faces looked taut and like plastic; under Hamed's beanie I could see half his hair had been burned off his scalp.

∾

Laila continued her rapid ascent on the viola, playing with more and more pride. She stood up straight, her chest proud. Her home life seemed to have stabilised somewhat and Jennifer had found out about a summer school at Yale University to which she was going to help Laila apply.

One day Laila came to her lesson morose and silent. She told me about her younger sister.

'Teacher Emma, my sister is so depressed. Her best friend was killed in Bamiyan. Now my sister sits alone at school. She always sat next to her friend. They loved each other, you know? Now she will not let anyone sit in her friend's chair. She is alone now.'

The genocide of the Hazaras continued, one little girl at a time.

∾

Finally, good news. The instruments that John and Liz and all their friends donated the money towards had arrived in Kabul. Now it would only take a ledger of paperwork to bring them to ANIM. The latest addition to the office, Mir Siraj Udin, was dispatched to customs to fill in multiple forms that would start the process of having the instruments released. Weeks passed; there was no sign of anything happening at all. I worried about the conditions the instruments were being kept in, hoping the cold wouldn't make the wood crack. We had dozens of string instruments waiting to be played and there didn't seem to be anything anyone could do. Mir Siraj Udin was spectacularly useless at his job and had failed the test twice to work at ANIM, but Dr Sarmast was given no choice: he had to be given the job because his uncle was a senior official in the education ministry. To release the instruments, Dr Sarmast finally brought out the big gun: Ustad Nader, the sergeant major teacher. Nader was a musician in the army band in the eighties and, even though his disciplining of the students was extremely harsh, clearly his military history had given him great training in how to get around bureaucracy.

The instruments arrived at ANIM the next day on the back of an open truck. The students rushed to help unload them. Sama itemised them and Koko Abdul unpacked the boxes with glee, holding the packing balloons in his mouth like a hungry clown and hurling them at me with as much violence as a half-inflated balloon can offer. Sydney Strings, where the instruments had been bought, had done an exceptional job with the packing and all the instruments were completely intact: baby violins,

violas, cellos and, the most beautiful thing of all, a baby bass.
John in particular had spent a huge amount of time organising
this, all the while fighting terminal leukaemia. These instruments were a testament to his generous, beautiful life.

$\approx$

End of year exams came around. The date for the exams was
set, then changed, then changed again. The total marks for
the exams were set, then changed again. It was like trying to
sit on a bucking horse and balance a ball on my head at the
same time. The situation was impossible, so I simply tried to
relax and accept. This was Afghanistan. It was as good as it
could be.

Most of my students were ready, apart from some seriously dodgy cases in the grade twelve ear-training class. In
the previous exams I had gone lightly on these students, but
now I knew the only way to be fair for the future of music
in the country was to sort the weak from the pretty good.
I prepared their exam sheets, tried to drill the students as hard
as possible and taught as well as I could. Some students, like
Meena, would excel. Others, like most of the grade twelves,
would probably fail.

During this time, a group of girls and teachers were on tour
to Germany with an organisation called Safar. This relationship
had been ongoing for a few years, and Afghan and German
musicians were to give concerts in Berlin and Weimar. I had
been due to be the girls' chaperone, but felt it was wrong
to go, knowing my true identity. I talked with Jennifer and

she offered to go instead; I would stay in Kabul and take her students through their exams.

The exams finally started and dragged on over two weeks; all academic subjects, then Western and Hindustani music theory and ear training.

The grade twelves sat themselves down in silence and I stood at the front with a metronome at the piano. I played eight-bar melodies for them to dictate, rhythms on a drum, and to finish they had to sight-sing melodies and rhythms individually. These young men really tried so hard. As they sang the melodies, their bass voices wavering on the high notes, I could see how much they had improved, but also how very far they still had to go. One young chap, Zial, couldn't even work out whether to go up or down. Others nailed the hardest intervals. Ahmad, the thrilling percussionist, was superb. He came from a famous musical family and you could almost see the music pouring from him. His grandfather had been playing at Radio Afghanistan when the Taliban reached Kabul. They came into the studio and broke his instrument in front of him; Ahmad's grandfather had a heart attack and died right there in the studio, beside his instrument.

Ahmad aced his exam.

Other students didn't do so well in their exams but excelled at trying to have their score changed. I had naively thought that corruption would end where music began. I was wrong.

One young man from grade fourteen, a saxophonist called Munib, had cheated. His sax teacher, Qasem, was in charge of music subjects and he stored the answers to all the exams in his cupboard. Allegra prepared her musical forms and analysis exam, gave the answers to Qasem, and delivered the exam to the students. She came back with curious results. Munib, not usually very good at this subject, had achieved a perfect score. On looking closer, she saw that his answers matched her own nearly word for word. It was clear that Munib had somehow taken, or had been given, the answers. I expected such a level of cheating to be punished by immediate dismissal from the school. This wasn't the case. Allegra had to write a new exam and Munib scraped a pass. He graduated to become a junior teacher at the school, presumably to hand on the same morals to a new generation.

Another student in grade six failed enough subjects to officially be dismissed from school. His father, clearly not happy, asked for the exams to be re-marked. Both Jennifer and Cami had pressure put on them by the principal to change their marks; they refused, knowing what a precedent this would set. It didn't matter what they thought. The principal, second in charge after Dr Sarmast and always a decent man, changed them anyway. The child stayed, to fail the next year and stay again.

And finally, the practical exams. This was my favourite time at ANIM. It was a chance to sit and listen and marvel at the achievements of these young people. Over this week I frequently had to fight back tears: seeing young women play rock and roll on a drum set with fierceness and attitude; watching a boy so small his feet couldn't reach the pedals play a Mozart piece on the piano; playing a duet with Meena and seeing the amazement on the other teachers' faces at how extraordinary she was. These were the very best of times at ANIM.

Dr Sarmast listened to many of the exams. He praised the students who had clearly practised, but the ones who clearly hadn't received the worst type of punishment: he simply and quietly showed his disappointment. It was highly effective. Negin, the pianist and conductor, played terribly. It was clear that all the attention she had received from the press that year in her role as conductor of the Afghan Women's Orchestra had not helped her studies at all, and nor had her split from Elham-Wickham. There was no need for any of us to tell her how badly she had done. She left the room sobbing.

One student, Mehran, had a very surprising exam. Mehran was the brother of Elham-Wickham and a very talented violinist. His brother had by now gained a place at Hunter College in New York and had been studying there since August. Mehran was exceedingly spoilt, both by his family and the school. It was a classic case of a person being good at something and their character being ruined by it. Mehran had been given clear instructions by Jennifer before she went to Germany about what to play in his exam, yet when the time came he pretended he had no scales or study to play. Usually he would earn a near-perfect score, but this time he barely passed.

His father, a famous singer, came to school the next day. I was pulled out of a lesson with Shaperai (who had passed her exam very comfortably) to go to a meeting with Dr Sarmast, Mehran and his father. I pulled on my hijab and sat down as Mehran accused Jennifer of not telling him what he had to play. I refuted this by showing them the documents Jennifer had prepared. There was no way out. The father tried to get Dr Sarmast to give Mehran a better mark; to ensure my respect for Dr Sarmast stayed intact, I never asked what he finally did. But I did know that Mehran was being allowed to saunter down a path that would lead to exactly the same place his brother had gone: musical success, character failure.

'Music exists to grow an admirable heart.' It was a quote from Dr Suzuki, founder of the Suzuki method, that sat at the bottom of every email from Jennifer.

Jennifer returned from Germany exhausted. We woke the next morning at 5 a.m. to rocket fire, immediate and deafening. It was an attack on an MP's house just a few streets away. I joined Jennifer to talk with her parents on Skype in New York state, trying to be breezy and brush off the obvious gunfire in the background. Afterwards I sat with Cami and Pancha in the garden. Cami looked defeated. He said this was it, it was all too much, that he was going to get a plane out that day. Cami had been under a huge amount of stress both at school and with his family: his wife had been applying for a green card in the US and it had only just been approved, he hadn't seen her for months, and he didn't know how he himself was going to be able to live with her. This level of horror so early in the morning was the thing that finally broke him. He calmed down, but I knew it was only a matter of time before

Cami left. The day started with gunfire and ended with an earthquake and a thunderstorm.

Cami was an exceptional musician and also very practical. When he had first arrived at ANIM he found three broken timpani abandoned at the end of a corridor. Cami examined them and worked out that, if he cannibalised one, he could fix the other two. At the next wind-band rehearsal he brought in the timpani and started to improvise a part, with Ustad Shefta conducting. After a few bars, Shefta stopped the orchestra, tears in his eyes. Shefta said that he had not heard this sound in thirty years. Cami was also an inspiring teacher. He had a very simple method: give a student a piece, tell them to practise it until they had memorised it, then give them a slightly harder one. Combine this with scales and studies and very quickly he had created some excellent percussionists. His studio was the most successful in the school and some of his students played at a level equivalent to any student in the world.

Oman was a great example. Oman was a quiet man in his early twenties and about to graduate from grade fourteen. He showed exceptional character, worked hard, and was not afraid to report things that might bring him a bad name. One time he had seen a sax student, Faisal, touch Mehran in a sexual way in a practice room. He went to Dr Sarmast and reported it. Dr Sarmast said he couldn't do anything as there was only Oman's word against Faisal's, but Oman had done the right thing. Oman stood slightly apart from the other students, a moral person.

For his graduation he had to play a one-hour recital. He practised until his hands had open sores. He wrapped them in bandages and continued to practise. He asked me to listen to his marimba piece and I was blown away by his skill and musicality, the most complex modern music played with four mallets twirling in his bandaged hands.

The day came for his recital. He had planned the pieces around a story of a percussionist being born and emerging slowly from behind a drum; it began with a simple drum piece then gradually moved to drum kit, marimba, then finished with the most thrilling snare-drum solo I have ever heard. The percussionist descended again behind the drum, back into the earth.

As he finished, the whole room erupted in applause. It was simply brilliant. The concept, the music, the performance, the effort. Oman received one hundred percent.

A few weeks later, Oman was in a bomb blast at the UN headquarters. He survived, but with injuries to his legs. He came to school the next day and carried on practising.

∽

Given the emotional suppression of everyone in Afghanistan, including teenagers, it was no surprise when certain things came to light at ANIM. I saw Faisal, the boy-man who had been with Mehran in the practice room, frequently appear threatening to younger boys. I heard rumours that Pedran, the cellist who had gone to France, had been molested by him. There were also rumours, never substantiated, of a female teacher starting relationships with older boys. Rumours, gossip, stories, but never any proof. I felt in my gut that some of these boy-men were definitely not to be trusted. I avoided being alone with most of them and made sure I was always closest to the door in a lesson.

All the teachers were ordered up to the staffroom one day in the middle of class. The students were left to their own devices as we all sat down, oblivious to the subject of the meeting.

What I heard was appalling and nearly beyond belief. Farhad, the dilruba player who had sat so close to frail old Professor Amruddin, had been taking photos of boys in the bathroom at ANIM then blackmailing them. Even though the students were supposed to hand over their phones when they arrived at school, Farhad had smuggled one in, engaged the help of two other boys and threatened mostly the grade sevens with the greatest of embarrassments. Dr Sarmast had possession of Farhad's phone, so the act was undeniable. This meeting was held for us all to vote on the fate of Farhad. There was no choice but to expel him, but there were two ways to do this. The first would be a dismissal that would allow Farhad to continue his education at another school (he was only in grade eight at this point). The second was to dismiss him with notification of his crime and he would end his education there and then.

There was no middle way.

I thought of how, if allowed, Farhad would continue his behaviour at the next school, and the one after that, continuing it all the way to manhood. I voted to have him expelled from the school system completely, for the sake of his potential future victims. Of course, this would also mean that Farhad's likely path would be to become even more criminal. It was a terrible choice. In the end, the majority voted to dismiss him with the chance of enrolling at another school.

I thought of Professor Amruddin, and his dilruba being smashed in front of him by the Taliban. Here was another destruction, but this time of the future of his instrument. Farhad had taken the trust of Amruddin and Dr Sarmast and smashed it in front of them.

Another devastation came quickly after: Ustad Mir Afghan, the tambour teacher, had been abusing his students during their lessons. The same grade seven boys. They had finally had enough and reported him to Dr Sarmast.

Mir Afghan was dismissed that day. At last, justice I could understand.

~

After a night out with a friend at Le Jardin, where acidic red wine was served in teapots, I returned home to find Cami and Jennifer huddled over something in the kitchen.

'What's going on, guys?'

'Look!'

And there on the floor was the smallest, grubbiest, most beautiful puppy in the world.

Cami had been home with Shazadah and had heard a yelp from a tree outside. He went to investigate and saw a bag thrown high into the branches. Out of the bag crawled a tiny dog. Cami had climbed up and rescued him, and now he was lying on the cushion, Pancha overseeing his care. The puppy was covered in red paint. Another victim of Afghan cruelty.

We decided he should go straight to Nowzad, the dog shelter. I brought him into my room, popped him next to Pancha on her cushion and woke up the next morning with him wrapped around my neck, his big brown Afghan eyes looking up at me.

And that (again) was that. We named him Perrito, Spanish for puppy.

~

Initially I told very few people about my decision to transition. Of course my big sister, Liz, was one, but my mum had to be the next.

'Binx,' said Liz, calling me by my family nickname, 'I'll tell her for you. The Internet is so crap, it would be awful if you told her and she said, "What? Trans what?" I'll tell her next Sunday and then we can call you after.'

I had loved my sister as much as I felt I could love anyone before this offer; afterwards, I understood how love has no limits.

That Sunday came, and Cami and Jennifer gathered to support me in case it all went horribly wrong. Mum had always been fine about Liz and me being gay, but this might push her over her eighty-one-year-old edge.

The FaceTime call came, the Internet for once good, the electricity constant. I saw Mum's face crooked on the screen. She burst into tears.

'Oh, Binx, why didn't you say something before? You must have been in so much pain.'

Another friend I told was Carol, a midwife in Brisbane. I had known her for years and we had become closer during my time in Kabul. Carol was one of the friends who stayed. I deeply treasured her regular support and news from home; Carol sent me photos from her life of beaches and forests and things that were only a memory in Kabul. We had talked in the past about my transitioning, but now I could tell her I had finally decided.

'Well, I know exactly who you should talk to.'

Carol's doctor in Brisbane, Leonie, had worked for many years in sexual and gender health. Leonie in turn referred me to Dr Gale Bearman, one of the leading transgender doctors in the country.

An appointment was set for the middle of December during the school's winter break. It was time to begin.

School ended with a meeting about the exams. All the teachers crowded into Dr Sarmast's room, apprehensive about what was coming. Dr Sarmast, so often calm, lost his temper. He banged his fists on his desk and yelled at us all for the disorganisation, the standard, our apparent lack of commitment, the sexual behaviour of the saxophone students. We sat in silence, knowing the best thing to do was to wait for Dr Sarmast's anger to blow over. Qasem, the sax teacher, knew he had to throw the attention elsewhere; he turned to me and criticised my students and their ability. I was devastated. Most of my students had worked so hard, I had worked so hard, and all my students had passed their exams, most with excellent marks. I understood how these accusations and the aggressive mood were nothing to do with me, but were symptoms of a deeper angst: Qasem about his own cheating with his student Munib; Dr Sarmast about going abroad so much to speak at conferences and receive awards; everyone about not being able to make the school better.

I couldn't wait to leave for Australia, to go back to a world of sense, clarity and safety. ANIM was as good as it could be, and that was hard to accept.

I returned to Brisbane, to the white summer light and buttery air. Carol took me into her care and fed me champagne and oysters and love. After the bitter Afghan winter, it was a renaissance.

I walked into Dr Bearman's office and took my first steps on my path to becoming the person I knew I was.

Dr Bearman asked me gentle, astute questions, talking about the various steps of treatment. She looked up and down at my androgynous figure and said, 'Let's face it, Emma. You won't need much tweaking.'

All natural things are coming

I returned to Kabul on 1 January 2016. Perhaps this would be the year when I would take proper control of my life. Perhaps, just perhaps, by the end of this year I would be nearer to my deepest desire, to be male in body and mind. And I would be able to stay in Kabul for one more year.

That afternoon I was tempted to go to Le Jardin for their new year dinner, but instead I napped with the dogs and woke to a distant explosion. A car bomb had gone off outside Le Jardin, killing two security guards and a twelve-year-old boy. Once again, luck had played the greatest part in my staying alive in Kabul.

∾

Every January and February, during the long break from school, ANIM had a winter academy. Most Afghan schools were closed for one simple reason: money. Heating them in the freezing winters simply cost too much, so students were expected to heat and educate themselves for three months until springtime and Nowruz, the Shia new year festival. ANIM students were a little more fortunate, although they now complained that they never had any time off. Winter academy included instrumental lessons, orchestra and revision of academic music subjects, plus English. It was basically school without the uniform or science. The lessons that Jennifer and I had planned for winter academy were given by Dr Sarmast, the male principal, Ustad Murat, and Sama. Covering etiquette, personal hygiene, how to talk with foreigners, and general decorum, these lessons worked a treat. There was a happier feeling throughout the school, almost as though the worst was behind us all.

Dr Sarmast had been trying for months, possibly years, to have the dusty schoolyard concreted and a basketball court built. Finally it was finished. Throughout winter academy, before school, at break, at lunchtime and for hours after school, the boys rolled up their sleeves and trousers and raced around the court, showing some serious athletic ability. One day after school I was chatting with Aziza and Nazira, watching the boys play.

'Girls, why should the boys always be the ones to have fun? Come on!'

And I dived onto the court, grabbed the ball and passed it to Nazira. It was like a beautiful fragrance blowing through the yard. Within minutes about ten girls had rushed onto the court, overwhelming the boys and passing the ball between them. They sprinted and threw and caught with glee, fierceness and a complete determination that no boy would ever tell them to leave that space again. It was possibly the best gift I ever gave them.

Winter academy was at its best in the weekly Wednesday concerts, when the Afghan instrumentalists in particular showed off their virtuosity. We had visitors from orphanages and charities and the audience went wild, listening to music from all around their country. Dr Sarmast invited master musicians from other provinces and continued his work of rebuilding Afghan music through sharing different traditions with the ANIM students. As the musicians started playing or singing, the whole audience clapped and danced and ended up giving standing ovations. I noticed that the Western music performed at these concerts didn't seem to bring the same joy, though. Was it the pace of the music? The unfamiliarity of it? The simple highlight for me was baby Meena playing 'Long, Long Ago' with Atesh. She smiled her dimple smile, sat down demurely, and played like a young Jacqueline du Pré, with a bow flourish at the end.

Winter was not as cold as usual, but the Taliban had developed a new strategy to make it as miserable as possible for as many people as possible. Along with blowing up the Internet cable from Pakistan and then laying landmines around where they had blown it up to slow down the repair, they had now blown up the main electricity line from Tajikistan. This meant that most people in Kabul had electricity only on alternate days. Allegra's day on was the Mexicans' day off, so we took it in turns to go round to each other's for dinner and stable illumination. Shazadah and Shersha kept us warm by lighting and stoking the bukhari heaters, and we spent most evenings sitting on cushions playing the board game Settlers of Catan and drinking you know what—whisky.

Once again, security had worsened. I wondered sometimes whether we were all boiling frogs, persuading ourselves that somehow things would get better. They didn't. There had been more kidnappings and, just before I returned from Australia, a murder. Lisa Akbari, an American–Afghan, had been working in Kabul for an NGO and was gunned down in her apartment complex. She was a friend of Jennifer's and had been at our house stroking Pancha just a few weeks before her death. Since a rumour was going around that Lisa had been killed for her Christian beliefs, I begged Jennifer to take out her crucifix earrings, for the sake of us all.

I had developed the small superpower of being able to sleep through distant bombs and not-so-distant gunfire, but one night in early January that power deserted me. Afghanistan had been playing a cricket match against Zimbabwe, it was down to the final few balls, and Afghanistan won. At around 11 p.m. that night I woke to rapid, very close gunfire, with what sounded like bullets ricocheting around our garden. I leapt out of bed, grabbed Perrito in my arms and Pancha by the scruff, and ran down to the safe room. Cami, Jennifer and Alex grabbed some water and food and tried to find out online what was happening. After about twenty minutes of continuous gunfire all around us, they discovered the most awful thing: all these bullets were in celebration of winning the cricket match.

Somehow, knowing this didn't make my heart slow down. It brought the heaviest misery down on me because, at that moment, I knew I would never, *never* understand Afghanistan.

This was only made worse the next day when Sama, the most reasonable person I knew in Kabul, laughed at us for being scared. The rocket fire had been Cami's turning point, and this was mine. At least one person died that night and many more were injured by stray bullets.

Winter was particularly hard for Jennifer, as she had to hop around on crutches after breaking her foot. It had happened just before our holiday, when she was standing on a chair to take a photo; the chair broke, Jennifer fell just a tiny distance, then came upstairs for a meeting with Dr Sarmast and suddenly burst into tears. I went to hospital with her and had the curious privilege of talking with the Afghan orthopaedic surgeon about breast augmentation and reduction in the West. Quite how we came to this conversation remains a mystery, but he was amazed that women could have their breasts reduced.

'But why would women do that?'

'Well, it can be very hard on their back . . .'

I then went on the explain bra cup sizes and (in a very inexpert way) how breasts could be made smaller.

'I am so shocked by this. In our country we don't have enough surgeons for anything, let alone breast reductions.'

This wasn't the first time Jennifer had broken her foot; she had arrived in the country over a year before on crutches.

After a blood test to check her vitamin levels at the French Children's Hospital in Kabul (well, Jennifer *is* small) it was revealed she had very low vitamin D, apparently extremely common amongst women in Afghanistan. Females spend most of their time indoors and when they do go out, they are completely covered, their faces and hands the only gateway to sunshine. Jennifer was fortunate and received a booster shot. Not the sort of shot people in this country always had.

Wais, our driver, had become an essential and much-loved part of our lives. Some Fridays he turned up at the Mexican House and cooked a breakfast of eggs and tomatoes, with the largest amount of garlic I have ever seen go into one dish. And then he did the washing up. Mrs Wais, a never-seen figure and his own 'her indoors', made vegetable dishes for us, which Wais delivered proudly—eggplant, green beans, and lubia, a red-kidney-bean dish made in a pressure cooker until the beans squish in your mouth. Divine food.

One morning there was less cheer. Wais arrived complaining of pains in his chest and down his arm. All of us immediately thought of a heart attack. Wais was an enormous man and his own father had died from a heart attack when he was very young. We insisted he go that very day to the doctor—and to a proper doctor, not one of the many shonky ones. We gave him some money and he reported back that afternoon: the doctor had diagnosed him with indigestion. Perhaps it was all the garlic. Wais' pain continued for the rest of my time in Kabul.

∽

As the winter academy went on and the electricity went on and off again, I received good news from Australia. When I had talked with Dr Bearman about treatment options, she suggested I consider having chest surgery (removal of my breasts and male contouring of my chest) first, to alleviate as much gender dysphoria as possible. This way, I could stay in Afghanistan for another year and wait more happily to begin testosterone treatment. It sounded like an excellent plan and she had recommended a surgeon in Brisbane, Dr Alys Saylor. Dr Saylor had an opening for surgery in the middle of February, the day before my birthday. It was perfect timing. I would have to miss the end of academy concert, but I would not miss too much teaching and could be back in Kabul close to the beginning of the school year in March.

At this point, you might be wondering what the difference is between being unhappy with your body in a general sense and gender dysphoria. I would venture that many people are unhappy with bits of their body, or perhaps all of it in terms of fitness or weight, but the distinct thing about gender dysphoria, at least for me, is that I hated the very expression of my body. It felt like I was trying to play a melody on my cello, but all the strings were badly out of tune and I had to constantly adjust, compromise, struggle. I hated my hairless face, my woman's voice, my hips, my female waist, even my hairline. This wasn't a weight or fitness issue; I had become very fit over the years, was strong and had low body fat. Rather, I felt like my body had committed treason against me. The most obvious signs of that were my breasts. If I could have waved a magic wand and become immediately, completely male, I would have done.

I now had the awful task of telling Dr Sarmast. I decided to be frank about the nature of the operation, but also decided he had no right or need to know the reason. I did my best to make it clear I was in no danger and that the operation was preventative (which it was), and was given leave to go for two months.

Dr Sarmast received more bad news—Cami had decided to leave ANIM. He needed to be with his wife and start his own process of applying for US residency, and the challenges of living in Afghanistan had finally defeated him.

Those challenges would defeat us all, at some point. Jennifer had put it perfectly: 'You know, I could live here so happily if just one thing were good—security, regular salary, teaching in a language I was fluent in, being able to plan for holidays, not having to redo work then having it ignored. But not one of those things is possible here.' Apart from everything else, Jennifer was once not paid for a whole six months.

My last concert was at the Russian embassy with Cami, Jennifer, Allegra, Diana the piano teacher and Ustad Shefta; this teachers' concert had become a regular winter event. We arrived at the embassy in the afternoon, had ourselves and our instruments thoroughly searched, and were taken into the embassy by the most glamorous woman I have ever seen, a Russian diplomat who looked like she had been transported direct from a Chanel showroom. I had tried to scrub up, but I lived in Kabul. She clearly didn't venture out much; you could tell from her shoes. We had prepared a concert of Russian favourites ('Moscow Nights', *Swan Lake*, Rachmaninov) with a little solo Bach from me and a Vivaldi violin concerto with Jennifer and Cami. The audience was made up of diplomats, high-ranking aid workers and more diplomats. They loved it. They particularly loved Jennifer with her Vivaldi and stamped their well-heeled feet for more.

After the concert the Russians served a buffet of caviar, smoked meats, rye bread and pickles. And vodka shots. I ended up drinking shots with Diana and a military attaché called Dmitri, then we Mexicans went home to drink more shots, without Dmitri. I would regret this (the shots, not the lack of Dmitri) the next day, as I could hardly stand from a hangover. Wais laughed hysterically at me, gave me a glass of lemon juice and drove very tentatively to the airport in case I threw up in his car. I stood in the car park where I had arrived nearly a year before and threw my arms around Jennifer, Cami and Wais. So much had changed, but so much more was about to change. I cried uncontrollably as Cami and Jennifer told me how much they loved me.

I took my first steps towards manhood. Hungover, wobbly ones, but at least going in the right direction.

∼

The sun was just coming up as the plane started its descent into Brisbane. British a cappella group Voces8 poured salve into my ears, singing John Williams's wordless lament 'Hymn to the Fallen'. Carol had offered to look after me during my recovery; she was a midwife and I was a curious, different baby, but being reborn none the less. This offer was an exceptional act of kindness and care. So many people who transition have no one to look after them; no one to wash them or cook for them or lift heavy things or watch TV with them or talk with them about their fears. The surgery meant that I wouldn't be able to even lift my arms beyond my shoulders for a month. Carol was my angel.

One of the requirements before having chest surgery is to get approval from a psychiatrist. I had been very lucky and, through Dr Bearman, had managed to get a Skype appointment with Dr Morris Bersin, a gender specialist in Queensland. I got up at 3 a.m. to speak with him, the Internet just strong enough to give us a video call for a few moments, then to audio. Dr Bersin asked about my earliest feelings of my gender, how that developed through my life, what support my family gave me, how I felt about my body, how I felt about my very self. It was a simple interview, because it was time. Some might say it was long overdue, but I believe that things come at the right time. Cami says that all natural things are coming, and he's Colombian, so he should know.

I truly had no doubt. In my sessions with therapist Adrienne (getting up at 4 a.m. every Friday to speak to her in Sydney) I had come to full acceptance of being transgender. Because it *was* an acceptance—there had never been a choice. In one of the sessions I told Adrienne about a dream I'd had: I was riding my motorbike around a city, half Kabul, half Sydney, and had stopped at a pub. There was a youngish man lounging on the window seat, wearing jeans and a t-shirt, smoking a fag and drinking a pint. I looked at him with great envy, and then I realised that I could do the same thing, there was nothing stopping me. So I went in, ordered a drink and inside were all my family and friends. They had all been waiting for me.

It is a simple dream to interpret: the man was me.

I sat in the waiting room at Brisbane Private Hospital, dressed stylishly in a surgical gown, cap and compression stockings. I was terrified. I was having a perfectly healthy bit of my body chopped off. The road ahead was completely hidden; this was a true step into the unknown. I had spoken to my mum the day before and she had cried. Then she said, 'Well, I think you are very brave.'

Liz had been more practical.

'Binx, you know you can change your mind. We won't think any less of you.'

I was so grateful for this, because it brought a final certainty.

Dr Saylor led me into a room to make the markings on my skin where she would cut. I stayed very, very still as she drew on me. I had been trying to build up my pectoral muscles as much as possible so that it would help with the positioning of the scars; the idea was for the scars to fade in under my eventually bigger chest, so the place where that pen went made a big difference.

It was time to go down to the operating theatre. I think I entered a different state here. In fact, I entered a state of grace. I had the most profound feeling of gratitude: gratitude that I lived in a country where being transgender is reasonably accepted, that I had Carol to look after me, that I had a family who loved me no matter what and friends who understood how vital this was for me, that I had money to pay for the operation (it was considered 'cosmetic', so not covered by the state) and time to recover. And I was finally grateful for myself. For being, after so many years and such great depression, brave. And, with this gratitude, I crossed over.

The day after the operation, on my forty-ninth birthday, I awoke with my new chest, a chest I had dreamt about having since I was twelve.

I stood up, helped by a nurse, and felt immediately the change in balance, the freedom, the loss. For months afterwards I would have phantom breasts in the shower, in bed, when I was walking down stairs. Dr Saylor came and examined the nipple grafts and pronounced me ready to leave hospital. I was squeezed and shoved into a compression vest by the nurse, given strict instructions not to take it off for five days and sent on my way, drains coming out my sides. Carol drove me home to pillows and fresh sheets and birthday champagne. It was my best birthday ever.

My wounds healed quickly with Carol tending to me. She surrounded me in beauty in every way: the food she made me, the music she played me, her kindness walking slowly beside me as I shuffled down the street, our little trips to beaches and forests. Finally, after eight weeks, it was time to return to Kabul. There was one more conversation to have.

During these weeks I meditated on what kind of person I wanted as a partner. I'd had so many relationships, but they had all ended badly, so I took this time to examine where I had gone wrong and how I might go right. And, after all this consideration, I realised my perfect partner had been with me all this time. Carol remains my perfect partner.

~

For the first time, returning to Kabul was very hard. I was aware of a huge reluctance: fear about security and my own teaching ability, knowing how hard the work was, and how things lived on the edge of nerves. I wouldn't see Carol for months and, although my chest was healed, the scars were still painful. Still, I had made a promise to Dr Sarmast and I was determined to keep it. I had to give myself a talking to. I can do this. I can bring joy. Do things one at a time. Work hard. Do my best. What else is possible?

I arrived back in early April, just a few days before Cami left for good. On the day before Cami's departure Atesh came to my room for our regular romp into the world of music and, really, everything. This day though, Atesh looked dreadful.

'Atesh, what's wrong?'

'Teacher Emma, I saw such a terrible thing on my way to school. There was a man lying in the street and he had blood pouring out of him. I think he had been stabbed. Teacher, I feel so bad. There was nothing I could do.'

What can anyone say to something like this? Because of the cultural restraints, I couldn't even hug Atesh. To salve his pain and bring him back to beauty, we listened to Arvo Pärt, our silence our balm.

That night we three Mexicans, Alex, Allegra and Shabheer had a final meal together.

Every evening, when Jennifer, Cami and I came home from school, we had sat outside with Pancha and a whisky and talked about the day. Jennifer introduced an idea that became incredibly important for all of our mental health—Good Bad Good. Each of us took it in turns to say one bad thing about the day, but, crucially, surround it by two good things. For sure, there were some days when it was hard to keep the bad thing to one, but there was never a day when we couldn't find two good things. In fact, every day offered more. It was so important because it reminded us all of the lessons we learnt in Kabul.

At our final meal, for us all, our goods were having the gift of teaching the children and having the gift of each other. There was no bad.

Cami left school sobbing his big, beautiful Colombian tears; he was whisked out of the gates by Wais, leaving behind a symphony of weeping. His departure was a huge loss both for the school and for the Mexicans. Cami was our calm, our centre, our wise person. I felt lonely without him, more than I expected. The same would have happened with Jennifer—it was the three of us that made it perfect. We were our own tripod.

Jennifer and I decided to move into a house with Allegra and Shabheer. Shabheer's visa was progressing well and they had decided to leave Afghanistan in August. If we all lived together we could save money and maintain the feeling of family. Shabheer, ever hard-working and organised, found a 1970s mansion for us right next to the vice-president's house, within its own security zone. Dr Sarmast was extremely unhappy with this and insisted we write a letter to the Ministry of Education, officially taking our security into our own hands. He warned us that the vice-president, a Hazara, was a major target for the Taliban and we would be in the firing line (literally) if he were attacked. This was true, but it would also be much harder to kidnap us with machine guns, concrete barriers and rocket-propelled grenades for protection. Before this we had only had toothless Shazadah and cute Pancha. Shersha took charge of the move and had made a new home for us by the time we got back from school the next day. He'd even made an apple cake. We named our new home the Colombian House, in honour of Cami.

With Cami gone, the students now had to pick up conducting the ensembles. Atesh and Qambar, a percussionist, conducted the youth orchestra and Negin continued with the girls' ensemble. At this point, Negin was probably the most famous girl in Afghanistan. Nearly every day journalists visited the school, all of them wanting to interview 'the girl conductor'. The BBC, CNN, various European and Australian news services. Negin was approaching the fame of Malala Yousafzai with her defiance of traditions and society.

Dr Sarmast was away for the first few weeks after I returned. His hearing had still not healed after the suicide attack at the French Cultural Centre and he stayed in Australia for check-ups. Finally, the day came for his return. Things always worked better when Dr Sarmast was around (although, when he was away, the school was also a lot calmer). Still, there was a funny feeling in the school over the few days before he returned. Two of my students, Nazira and Hafizah, had missed their lessons and, when I saw them, they appeared extremely distracted. When I asked them what was happening they avoided my gaze, shrugged and mumbled, 'Nothing, teacher.'

When a student says that, you know the exact opposite is true, but no matter how much I asked, no one would tell me what was disturbing the older girls. It wasn't just Nazira and Hafizah. Gulalai and Houma, both sitar players and usually gleeful and open, now huddled endlessly in corners, whispering with Hafizah. This wasn't just light gossip. Their faces looked strained, as if there was a great moral decision they had to make. Whenever I walked near, they stopped talking and waited until I went past. It felt awful to not be able to help them. I was clearly a foreigner, in every way.

I was teaching a theory class in a room facing the main gate when, just after 1 p.m., Wais' car appeared through the gate with Dr Sarmast in the back. Wali and Naeem, the gate men, shook and kissed his hand. My students squealed with anticipation and wanted to go and greet him, but I asked them to wait for the end of the lesson, as that was what he would have preferred. Just after Dr Sarmast came into the building,

I noticed an older girl—let's call her Yalda—run across the schoolyard. She had a strange look on her face, which at the time I took for excitement. She hurried into the building and I continued with our lesson on melody composition (big tip: don't use too many notes).

Suddenly there was a rumble of sound from the corridor. This could have been anything, so I ignored it. News would get out sooner or later about what had happened and I was so tired of gossip. I gave the students their homework (write an eight-bar melody with a harmonised cadence) and went out into the corridor. It was a step into perdition. Dr Sarmast was screaming instructions. Girls were weeping. Boys stood around looking embarrassed. And then I looked outside. Yalda was being carried to Wais' car and she was screaming.

I found Jennifer in her room and asked her what on earth had happened. It was like hell had descended on the school. All she knew was bad enough—Yalda had fallen out of the first-floor bathroom window and was going to hospital. But it would get far, far worse than that.

I was confused about how Yalda could have fallen from the window. It was high and would have taken great effort to even climb up to it. As the hours went by and school finished, bits of news slowly came together until, by the end of the day, a hideous, truly tragic story was formed, its warped shape forever a shadow on all our lives.

The apparent 'truth', the Afghan truth, was this: Yalda had begun a relationship with Sameem, the junior tabla teacher. This was not news. In fact Jennifer, Allegra and I had all advised

Yalda against spending so much time with boys in general, and particularly Sameem. Yalda had shrugged me off, saying the boys came to her, so what was she to do?

'Tell them to go away and do their own practice, and you will talk to them later. Yalda, you must take charge of your own time, otherwise you are wasting your life. And you must think of your reputation.'

Yalda continued to spend every break, and many practice sessions, with Sameem. Their relationship had been going on longer than anyone knew; just after another friend had left Afghanistan, Yalda in a fit of pique had taken photos on her phone of herself and Sameem kissing. Also one of herself naked. She had then put these on a USB drive, perhaps forgotten they were there and lent the USB drive to a grade twelve boy-man percussionist, Meehran. He was supposed to just take a music file from the drive, but had looked through it and found the photos. Meehran in turn showed another student, Elias (one of my bass students), and so the photos had made their way through the senior boys at school. The older girls somehow found out about them and that is what they had been discussing in the days leading up to this awful incident. They were trying to decide what to do about Yalda; she had brought shame upon them by behaving in such a way and they had to do something to protect their own reputations.

You may think that having a photo of yourself kissing someone is not too bad, but in fact there isn't really an equivalent in Australian society. Perhaps the closest might be if you had bestial sex and videoed it. Even that doesn't get to the heart of the shame Yalda had brought upon herself and the school.

The older girls had decided to get a copy of the photos from one of the boys, tell Sheba, the female principal, and see what she said. Less than an hour before Dr Sarmast returned, less than an hour before someone with great sense and logic could deal with the issue sensitively, Hafizah and Sheba confronted Yalda about the photos. She ran from the room, which is when I saw her looking so strange running across the schoolyard. She went up to the bathroom and threw herself out of the bathroom window.

Jennifer and I sat in my room, utterly spent by the day's horror. Dr Sarmast came in and sat down with us. His face was unlike I had seen it before, even during times of great stress. He simply had a look of not knowing what to do. He looked lost, morally lost.

'Dr Sarmast, what are you going to do?' I asked. 'Will you sack Sameem? The boys must be punished for showing these photos around. Surely this is illegal here.'

All the indignation and anger that had built up over my time in Kabul came out in a massive, unfettered rage. In Yalda's story I saw the ills of Afghan society as a whole. This young woman was living in the twenty-first century in a country that had received billions of dollars in aid for over a decade. She had studied music for years, gone abroad, she was officially an adult, and yet, and yet, and fucking yet, she was still treated like chattel. Like her actions demonstrated a truly evil person, rather than a young woman who had simply been in love. Her treatment was that of a woman in the Middle Ages. If the men were not punished, it would be as it always was: the woman would take the punishment and the shame and have to hide herself forever. And the men would go on treating women as objects, ridiculing them, mocking them, ruining them. It made me feel physically sick then, and, as I write this, it does now. Yalda had fallen, literally and metaphorically, yet the fault lay entirely in other people's hands.

Dr Sarmast truly did not know what to do. If he punished the boys properly he would have to bring in the police. He would be able to sack Sameem more easily, but there was also the problem of Sheba and Hafizah. Under Afghan law, if someone drives a person to attempt suicide they can be prosecuted.

Basically, for the people responsible for Yalda's suicide attempt to be properly punished, ANIM would face enormous scrutiny, possibly even closure. And ANIM was too big, too important, to fail. The World Bank, the US embassy and other donors had poured millions of dollars into ANIM. The school was one of the few demonstrations of success in the decade-long war in Afghanistan, a conflict that had led to failure in so many ways. It was simply too hard to admit that this too might have failed, that Dr Sarmast's ambition of having a music school that taught not only Afghan music but Western music as well, with girls and boys equal, was simply too big a step. Would it have been better to open an Afghan music school, then build on top of that? Perhaps that would not have brought in all those donors quite as keenly. In any other country, ANIM would be a resounding success and, indeed, in Afghanistan it brought joy and hope to many, but it was a perpetual target of conservatives. And in the five years since its foundation, at the time of writing, only two girls had graduated. And the others? The missing girls? Like Sonam the viola player, like Tahmina the clever violinist with a gossiping brother, they had been taken and locked up in a prison of propriety.

All this played out around the same time as the Royal Commission into Institutional Responses to Child Sexual Abuse was interviewing Cardinal Pell. The parallels were clear and undeniable. To save the Catholic Church, legions of lives had been ruined. To save ANIM, it seemed Dr Sarmast gave himself no choice but to keep the story of Yalda a secret.

How can we judge? How can we truly understand Dr Sarmast's decision? I see now that I never can. And, unless you have grown up in that country and tried to do what Dr Sarmast achieved, you never will.

The next day news came of Yalda's injuries. She had been lucky, only breaking a foot and damaging a number of discs in her back. She was taken to an aunt's house in Kabul and the family told she was simply distraught over the recent death of her grandmother.

With the virtuosity of gossip in the school, it was no surprise that everyone knew Yalda's story by the next morning. The hardest moment was in girls' ensemble. I stood up and spoke to the girls. I can't remember what I said now, but I do remember Jennifer's face as she listened to me. I could see that she was grateful for a change in mood, for some humour and lightness amongst such ghastliness. After an hour or so, the students returned to the place that had always given them shelter—music.

~

The only person to behave in a way I respected and could understand in these days was Atesh. This dear, beautiful boy cried about Yalda. He had tried to be a good friend and help her with her playing and academic work, but she had been too caught up with love. Atesh understood this, forgave her and only wanted to help her. Other people blamed Yalda solely. Shaperai talked with me about Yalda and what a bad person she was.

'Shaps, Yalda is not a bad person. She made a mistake. And, you know, we will all make mistakes. We have to show compassion.'

Shaperai bowed her beautiful head and nodded.

Hafizah didn't seem to have learnt anything from the tragic results of her gossip. Laila came to my room one day, crying because the US embassy had cancelled her visa appointment to go to Yale for summer school. Her mother had no money and she had had to walk two hours to the embassy, for no purpose. Once again, I held Laila as she wept. Hafizah came up to me afterwards, a pernicious look on her face, and asked why Laila was crying. I was incredulous. I snapped at her, told her it was absolutely not her business and to stop gossiping. Hafizah never really talked to me after that.

Dr Sarmast finally sacked Sameem. Nevertheless, Sameem hung around school over the next few days, laughing with the older boys. It was all I could do not to punch him in the face. I have never been so viciously angry. Dr Sarmast tried to investigate the source of the photos' distribution, but nobody was ever punished. All the boy-men involved stayed at school, even Meehran, the supposed source of the photos. I couldn't look these boys in the eye. I was especially angered by Samir, who had put the photos on his own USB drive. I knew how kind he could be, but if this crime went unpunished how would he ever make his way in the world? Who was to be his guide?

I felt enormous guilt over all that happened with Yalda. If I had had a closer relationship with Nazira, Hafizah and Elias maybe, just maybe, they would have told me what was going on and I could have advised them to wait and tell Dr Sarmast. But I didn't have that relationship. I was a foreigner and even foreigners such as Allegra, who was so dearly loved by the students, didn't know what was happening. It finally became clear that I could never be the teacher I wanted to be for these people.

Just because one awful thing had happened didn't preclude other awful things happening. Murzghan, a teenage percussionist, had been extremely vague at school. I taught her Western theory and she often came late, or not at all, to class. It turned out that her family had taken her out of AFCECO, the 'orphanage', to live again at home. But her mum had a new husband and Murzghan was dumped on the street. She went to her dad's mother, who in turn threw her out, since Murzghan's mother had a new husband and had therefore disgraced the family. Murzghan went to a mosque as a last resort; luckily another ANIM student saw her there and took her to their family. Dr Sarmast intervened and arranged for her to go back to AFCECO.

I would never truly know the stresses these kids were under.

Laila reported that her mother had told her she was the cause of her problems.

'Teacher Emma, people here eat you with their words.'

One day she missed school because now her foot was hurt and she couldn't walk the distance. She said how stressed her mother always was, and how she was so often ill. Laila often felt better if I managed to bring a scientific explanation to a problem, so I talked about how intergenerational stress could be passed down through DNA.

'You know, Laila, how foreigners often look much younger for their age than Afghans do? It's not just diet; it's because you have to live with so much stress, and the stress of generations before you.'

This distracted Laila's mind a little from her troubles; a tentative light returned to her face.

Marjan, the green-eyed violinist, came late to school with her sister. They also lived in a faraway suburb and had to walk to school because their mother, the sole breadwinner for the family, had been diagnosed with a brain tumour and couldn't work. Jennifer and I chipped in for bus fares and Marjan looked away, ashamed.

'Thank you, Teacher Jennifer, Teacher Emma.'

~

In these days I needed to protect the babies as much as possible. I kept their lessons light and fun and easy. Meena came to her lessons with worry on her forehead, developing her own Kabul Eleven. We sat together and played duets, Meena now able to play Bach minuets, change left-hand positions and even do vibrato. Vibrato for the cello is usually taught much later, but Meena was special. She copied me as I played and any faults she had were simply because I have them myself. Meena had memorised the whole of the first Suzuki book in less than a year. She played in tune with a big sound, a variety of dynamics and great sincerity. Very soon she would be the best cellist in Afghanistan. She would have been a delight to teach anywhere, but in Kabul Meena was heaven-sent. I prayed that she would be able to join her older sister in Germany and have Beethoven and Bach with her every day.

∾

Rehearsals went on, school went on, lessons went on. News of Yalda came occasionally and then I heard that she had come to school and was in Dr Sarmast's office. I raced up the stairs, needing to show her how much I cared for her. Because of her back pain she seemed to hover over the chair, a tiny, weak, wrecked girl. She looked like she was still in shock. Her skin had once been rosy, but now it was grey. Her pride, her fierceness, her power, they had all been flayed from her. I hugged her gently, stroked her hand and cried with her. And then I left. I knew there was nothing else to do.

I continued to talk with Dr Sarmast about what to do with the boys who had stolen the photos. I reminded him that, even though I would never understand Afghanistan and its society, still there were universal truths to consider: the rights of Yalda; that truth will out; that a wrong must be punished. After a moment of thought he agreed, then went back to the Afghan way. It was clear he could and would do nothing.

In the end, Meehran decided for himself. He paid US$4000 for a Turkish visa that should have cost US$100. He left, believing he could get a scholarship to go the US and train to be a pilot. Perhaps he could. Perhaps he will. Perhaps he will fly around the world, forever ignorant of what he has left behind.

∿

After such a living nightmare, there had to be good news. There *had* to be. And finally there was. Baset had raised all the money he needed for his visa to Interlochen Center for the Arts in Michigan and now was waiting for the result of his visa interview. I asked him every day for news. I was so worried that Fayez and Milad's staying in New York would ruin Baset's chances. He came running to me one day after school, before chamber orchestra rehearsal.

'Teacher Emma, I have my visa. I am going to the United States.'

∿

All this time of horror had taken its toll on my health. A shadow of my shingles from many years ago burnt along my optic nerve; my chest scars pierced my skin and rose up raw and red every night. I had reverted to wearing my compression vest for comfort, like an autistic child in a Temple Grandin machine. Carol was beautiful and calm and said whenever I needed to come home, that would be okay. I had just signed another contract promising Dr Sarmast I would stay another year, but I knew I couldn't do it. I couldn't stay in this school and be party to the silence over these boys' abuse of Yalda. I couldn't stay and teach these students, many of whom now clearly didn't respect me as anything beyond a cello teacher, and sometimes not even that.

After Yalda's suicide attempt, my own feelings were impossible to hide. I felt so much contempt for the older boys, and hated myself for feeling that way. They saw my hatred and all the older boys now avoided me, or spoke to me very rudely. I hated the foolishness of the female principal and I was angry at Hafizah for confronting Yalda in such a brutal way. I couldn't stay in a place where bombs went off every day and kidnappings were becoming more and more regular. I couldn't stay in a place where people thought it was funny to shoot bullets into the air and murder small girls and never tell the truth. There were kids in Australia who needed a cello teacher too. And I realised that it was time to start taking testosterone. I knew that I couldn't be here and transition, yet I couldn't *not* transition. All of these reasons, but one above all: I had lost hope for Afghanistan.

I simply told Dr Sarmast that I needed to return home for my health. He was perfectly accepting.

'Ms Ayres, your health must come first.'

My students were either devastated or nonchalant. They had seen this before—foreign teachers often came and left, but at least I had not left in the middle of the night, like some did. Atesh and Nazira were crestfallen. When I broke the news, I felt as if I was inflicting a terrible injury on them. Sultan, the brilliant tabla and double-bass player, gave the most crushing response.

'Teacher, you should never have come.'

The school was critically wounded and we needed a salve. True to Afghanistan's mystery, it came in the form of a poet: Massoud Khalili. Even his name was poetic. Khalili was the son of a man with an even more poetic name, Khalil Khalili, the greatest Afghan poet of the twentieth century. Massoud Khalili had his own wounds to salve; he had been standing beside Ahmad Shah Massoud, commander of Northern Alliance, when he was assassinated; his face was heavily scarred, one eye blind. Massoud had been the one man in Afghanistan who had a hope of uniting the country. Two days after he was assassinated, the World Trade Center buildings in New York were destroyed by two planes flying into them.

It was announced that Khalili would be visiting the school the next day, just a few days before I was due to leave. One thing ANIM did brilliantly was put on a good show at a moment's notice. Dr Sarmast summoned all the teachers to discuss the visit, and Ustad Wali, the English program co-ordinator made a timetable of events. Each ensemble was to play a piece for our guest, he would visit each teacher's studio to hear individual players and the climax would be a performance by the Afghan Youth Orchestra.

I had a new student called Besheda and I chose her as my demonstration, mainly because she had missed a few lessons, but also because of her background. Besheda lived in an internally displaced persons camp on the outskirts of Kabul. I had never visited these camps, but a friend had described them as the poorest, most wretched places in the world. Besheda attended school with her older brother. She was a ferocious little girl, in a similar mould to Fatima, and was stubborn and quick. One Saturday, after our single day off, I asked her if she had had a good day on Friday.

'No, teacher, no. Fridays I don't like. I have to work. Washing, cleaning, cooking.'

I could see it in her hands, which were covered in red cracks and callouses; she had the hands of a slave. I never asked Besheda about Fridays again.

We were working on the American folk song 'Go Tell Aunt Rhody'; I told Besheda about the important person coming and said that we would play the piece through. We hadn't actually managed to do it up to that point, but I said that, if she went wrong, she should try to keep going. In the wise words of Jennifer, if she missed a note, it was gone forever.

Dr Sarmast and Ustad Wali came into the room with Khalili. He was a terrifying, magnificent-looking man, the sort who immediately makes you try to be as good as you possibly can be. Besheda must have thought this too, because she played like a newborn star. She was flawless and at the end smiled beatifically at her audience. I wasn't sure who was the more impressive now, this little girl or the war veteran. Khalili kissed Besheda's forehead and uttered poetry that only an Afghan could speak convincingly.

'Child, you should thank your teacher a million times for being here. If I had time I would.'

Up to this point, I had been happy with my decision to leave Kabul. This moment nearly broke my resolve. I felt ashamed of my choice; I felt selfish, shallow and weak.

Things only got more emotionally intense as Khalili's visit went on. I applauded and thanked Besheda and rushed down to take my place with Laila and the Afghan Youth Orchestra.

This was the last time I would play with the orchestra. The room was packed; everyone was there except, of course, Yalda. Atesh and Qambar conducted and we played Afghan music, arranged by Allegra. I had never heard the orchestra sound so good before. The strings section, since Jennifer's and my arrival, had doubled. Their sound was bold and warm and thick; it had a depth and an integrity I had never heard before. The winds played with clarity and unity and the Afghan instrumentalists, at the feet of the conductor, struck their instruments with a passion that was clearly inspired by this day and this exceptional man. I heard for the first time that they had taken into their hearts the basic tenet of orchestral playing: the whole is more than the individual parts. If this was the only thing they learnt from ANIM, all our jobs had been done.

One of the pieces we played was 'Pa Loyo Ghro Bande', which was my absolute favourite of anything we played. Allegra had the talent of bringing a sweet melancholy to a piece with her harmonies and placing of the different instruments. This particular song was a dance, an attan. It is a slow dance, perhaps like a sarabande, but with seven beats in each bar. I had watched the most masculine of men perform the dance at a party, their guns put aside, their beards and arrogance completely subsumed by this restrained dance. But an attan was hard to play—it needed to be held tight by the conductor, standing upright in its flow, its feet light yet firm on the ground. The orchestra so often raced ahead in this piece and its beauty was trampled, but on this day they played with extraordinary grace.

Qambar was a brilliant conductor, with a natural arrogance and command. He had once turned to me in orchestra and said, 'Teacher Emma, have you heard of a singer called Elvis Presley? He is really good!'

Qambar was eighteen and the year before had married his brother's widow, who already had one child. He was no boy-man—he was a man, and it showed in how he controlled the orchestra.

Khalili was clearly deeply moved. There was silence when we stopped, even from the players. We all somehow knew that this performance was the one that had healed the school's wounds. Khalili then spoke to us, as only brilliant orators can, individually and yet together. He spoke of hope and love and how they are the only two things you need in your heart and your head. And that the sound of music is the sound of the door to paradise. I fought back my tears as he spoke.

Maybe, in this crazy, fucked-up place, music really could fix everything. And when there is so much despair, what else can we do but play?

Khalili allowed my love and compassion for these young Afghans, for Afghanistan itself, to flourish again. I returned to my room with Jennifer and we fell into each other's arms, sobbing.

Afghanistan overwhelmed me to my core. It fundamentally changed my view of the world. It was full of the best and worst of life and there was never any middle ground. I came from a temperate land and I needed something less manic, but this country had taught me to love intensely and to not be afraid of living at the extreme. I was like a Picasso painting, taken apart and put back together in a new, strange form. What a gift.

Silver boxes

lay on my bed, the early summer sun falling through the curtains. Pancha barked lazily outside and one of Allegra's cats, Eidie, sat purring on my stomach. The muezzin called for prayer from the old mosque behind our house and I pictured Shabheer in his room, taking his prayer mat and bowing to God. A soft sheet of stillness lay over Kabul, the city quietened by Ramadan.

My room, always spartan, was now nearly empty. I wouldn't need any long, feminine shirts anymore, so had given most of my clothes to Shazadah to sell for himself. The rest of my things had been packed up, ready to be shipped back to Australia.

Shazadah sat in his room at the back of our house, listening to the radio. He couldn't read, but he loved listening to music. He was crying.

'Shazadah, what's wrong? Can I help you?'

'Mr Emma,' he said (I had always been Mr Emma to him), 'you are going, Allegra and Shabheer are going, Jennifer is going. I will have no work again. I must have money for my family.'

Everything he said was true. Jennifer had decided to leave in July and the next foreign teachers might not want to live in our house, so we couldn't promise Shazadah more work. There were thousands and thousands like Shazadah, Afghans who had earned a good living working for foreigners, but now most of the foreigners had gone.

And the tears, from this toothless, kind, middle-aged film-star boy from a tiny Afghan village continued to fall.

That night we hosted a concert at our house. A trio of musicians from Australia, the String Contingent, was visiting ANIM and they were coming to play, along with Ustad Rameen on rubab, the two Indian classical teachers, Abhishek and Murchana, and Professor Korevaar from Colorado. He had been Allegra's teacher at college, so there was a particular importance to his visit.

Shabheer told Allegra and me about a special lamb dish where the whole lamb, stuffed with rice and spices, was cooked in a clay oven for eight hours. I suspected such a dish would be hard to find in Australia, so we ordered one and had it delivered. Shershah made another trifle, Shabs brought some soft drinks and we were ready for a party.

A soirée. It was an unlikely place for a soirée, in a country where music was often shunned, in a house next to the vice-president of the whole country and surrounded as we were by enough weaponry to start a civil war. We invited Dr Sarmast, Ustad Shefta, Shersha, Shazadah, a few foreign friends and a couple of missionaries who had just arrived. If I had known they were missionaries before they came I would have protested, as they were often the targets of attacks, but this night was clearly blessed.

The concert began with Professor Korevaar playing Schumann and Chopin on Allegra's electric keyboard. Then the String Contingent with folk-inspired groove, the Indians and two classical ragas, and finally Ustad Rameen with awe-inspiring virtuosity in his Afghan music. Shabheer had made a small stage for them from a table and the audience surrounded it on cushions.

It was, for me, the epitome of a concert. The audience and the players were as one and the music flowed from one style to another, a reminder that music unites us all, no matter our nationality or education or class or age or belief. *This* was the Afghanistan Dr Sarmast was fighting for, and, in this night, we all saw his dreams come true.

There were two more concerts to play before I left. The first was a joint concert with the US Army 10th Mountain Division Band, who had flown in especially from Bagram Air Base. They arrived with their instruments and their rifles, looking precise and shorn. Shabheer had lent Atesh his special music-notation tie and Atesh held it out to me.

'Teacher Emma, I don't know what to do with this. Can you make it for me?'

He turned around and I tied his tie for him from behind, like a father for his son.

The ANIM students loved being with the American soldiers. Baset the trumpeter particularly, as he was invited to play with them in the 'Bugler's March'. Then there was the wonderful realisation by the students that the music they played, in these odd bars of five or seven beats, was extremely hard for Western-trained musicians. They could do something better than the Westerners. We performed a few Afghan pieces together and, for the climax, Sousa's 'The Stars and Stripes Forever'. As the final refrain came round, the whole orchestra stood up and played, even Nazira, Hafizah and me. Sousa's music was taken into a whole new world by the Afghan instrumentalists, who somehow made the regular four beats in a bar sound like seven. No matter the place, no matter the occasion, Afghans would do what they wanted.

I had given my notice to finish just after the chamber orchestra concert at the Swedish embassy for their National Day. Allegra and I had arranged some Swedish music, including a few tunes by ABBA.

Aziza was playing double bass beside Sultan in 'I Have a Dream'.

'Teacher Emma, do you have a dream?'

Rehearsals were so-so until I showed the musicians a video of ABBA playing 'Mamma Mia'. The video was direct from the seventies, with Anni-Frid and Agnetha wearing very, very tight white jumpsuits that left absolutely nothing to the imagination, especially not a teenage boy's imagination. Following this, the speed and the vigour of their playing improved exponentially.

It was my final day at school. After this day I could allow my outside to match my inside. I could put myself in tune.

I left my teaching room for the last time. The music that had been played there, the musicians created and improved, the laughter, the weeping, the scowls, the mind-opening acquisition of knowledge, the ultimate joy of being able to play an instrument: all that had happened in my little room in the west of Kabul.

We packed our instruments onto an open truck and stuffed ourselves into the school bus. Dr Sarmast had recently disciplined Ustad Nader and the bus driver for cooking their lunch inside it, and the smell of Kabuli pilau still lingered. We followed the truck through Kabul, past the place where Farkhunda was murdered, past the markets and shrines and checkpoints, past a beggar with no hands, into the green zone. The sight of a truck with two double basses sticking out of it didn't seem to bother anyone. Perhaps the bus full of Afghan Kuchis, or nomads, who were actually playing as they overtook us, had stolen our thunder. I sat beside Medina, sang songs with her in solfège and tried to soak every moment into my memory.

It took ages to get everybody through security. While we waited, Atesh, in his concert tails, chatted to a security guard, his machine gun pointing at Atesh's heart. Finally we were all through and we stepped into that other world, the world of embassies and perfect grass and people who could leave whenever they wanted.

We set up the orchestra under an awning and waited for the guests to arrive. Amazingly everyone came on time, even the Afghan VIPs, and the concert began. We had planned to have a few duets with the Afghan instrumentalists first, then move into the full orchestra pieces. We had been warned that people would be 'mingling' in the first part, but we didn't anticipate just how much they would mingle. And talk. And how little they would listen. Gulalai and Houma began with a short Indian raga and the audience talked. Nobody clapped at the end, so I started the clapping for them, to remind them of the work we had put in and the beauty they were missing. It didn't make any difference. These young musicians were amazed that nobody wanted to, was not compelled to, listen to their music. Sultan, playing double bass, turned to me. 'Teacher Emma, why is no one listening?'

'Because they're diplomats, Sultan. Their world is talking. We're doing what musicians all around the world have to do to make money. We're playing background music.'

The diplomats missed so much that day. One of the rubab players, Samim Zafar, was a truly brilliant musician. Most Afghan music is developed melodically, rather than harmonically like Western music, but Samim had developed a style of composition where he managed to do both. The rubab had been laughed out of the Indian court back in the 1700s for being too crude an instrument, but in Samim's hands I believed it could describe the world in its sound. He played his own composition with Masjedi on cajón drum, and afterwards Nazira and I played a Vivaldi duet.

Nazira was a completely different player from when I first arrived. She had developed a great subtlety of phrasing and sound, had better rhythm and intonation and was beginning to really meld into her cello. She loved her cello, just as baby Meena loved hers. These girls were true musicians.

Nazira had been working on a Vivaldi sonata and played it for her practical exam. She received full marks because she had taken the music into her body and spirit. She sang this music on the cello, so we planned to play it for all the dignitaries that day; surely these cultured people would be the best to appreciate her achievement. We started to play and the chatter from the audience increased. We played louder. They talked louder. Louder and louder, until the sound system started to shriek with feedback. The sound guy, Ustad Basir, the lazy guitar teacher, had failed to show up for the concert and Masjedi and Samim Zafar were doing their best to control the microphones, but it only got worse. And then, the ultimate humiliation: a diplomat from somewhere walked up to us and told us to stop playing. Nazira burst into tears and ran from the stage.

From the micro to the macro: what happened with the musicians in ANIM could always be taken as a wider lesson in Afghanistan's fate. Nazira had practised for endless hours and put everything into her performance, but a teacher's failure to show up and the diplomats' self-interest meant that she would never be heard. I could see why she was left completely desolate by the man's words. It was an experience that she would probably never truly recover from.

We all, teachers and students, tried to comfort her and explain the man's inexplicable actions. She eventually came back to the stage in time for the full orchestra pieces, tears still in her blue eyes. Again the audience failed to listen, but this time none of us cared. We played all the pieces we had spent dozens of hours rehearsing and applauded ourselves instead. Jennifer stood up at one point and reminded everyone that this was my last concert.

Qambar, conducting, turned to me. 'Teacher, we will play for you.'

Curiously, after all the music was finished, a few guests stayed behind and insisted we play again. So Atesh picked up his baton and we played. We were the Afghan Chamber Orchestra and in that moment, despite the crazily fast speeds and everything that had happened before, I wouldn't have wanted to be anywhere else.

~

I woke the next morning at 4 a.m. to catch a plane to Bamiyan with my mate Charlotte and the photographer Andrew Quilty. To celebrate my first step into manhood I wore my favourite shirt, jeans, boots and no hijab. At the airport, in the need to start my new life, I perhaps recklessly joined the male line to be searched, unsure what would happen if they found out. The Afghans weren't convinced. A female police officer came up to me and asked if I would like to join the women's line.

I declined, hoping there wouldn't be too much groping around the groin for the body check. The male security guard frisked me lightly; I think he didn't want to discover my physical truth. I resigned myself to having to live in the middle for a while longer. Carol had booked an appointment for me with Dr Bearman on my return to Brisbane, but I would have to wait endless weeks until then for my first shot of testosterone.

Bamiyan somehow filled in the gaps for me that were left from Kabul. Which was ironic, considering Bamiyan itself was famous for two very large gaps: the caves where the two Buddhas of Bamiyan had once reared so magnificently for over a thousand years. The Taliban had destroyed the Buddhas in 2001, but they had had to work hard at it. First tank shells, then artillery shells, then the final coup de grâce: bombs planted directly around them. In classic Afghan style, no one could now agree how the Buddhas would be rebuilt, so the holes where they once stood remained.

I sat for hours staring at these two gaps from my hotel balcony. Images tumbled through my mind of their construction, the thousands of monks who once lived there, the brutality of the Taliban, then the years of neglect of the Hazara people who lived there. I tried to equate the loss of the Buddhas in musical terms, but all I could come up with was a concert hall full of people waiting to hear Beethoven's Symphony No. 5 and only silence endlessly performed for them.

We three walked around freely and safely. We ate Japanese food and I happily stopped drinking alcohol—the first time for many, many months. The air was pure and vital, the fields were green, the streets were clean, the houses unencumbered by barbed wire, the people openly friendly. Something, though, didn't sit easily within me. Then it dawned on me that I actually didn't know how to walk through the world as a man. I was a man, but in many ways a proto-man. I was no longer in the middle, the place I had occupied for all my life. Now I was teetering towards the edge and it became scarier every day. I tried to copy Andrew's mannerisms, dress, walk, his air. Since I hadn't learnt how to be a man as I grew up, I had to choose how to be my own man now, but at least I would learn from the men I wanted to learn from.

Being transgender is like walking on a tightrope, and I had to hope that the rope would slowly get wider and turn into a path, a road. I knew that if I looked down now, I would fall. I had to keep following my inner compass; I had to keep my head up.

A rainbow appeared above the caves. There is an Afghan belief that if you cross through a rainbow, you become the opposite gender.

~

Allegra, Shabheer, Jennifer and Alex joined me for early-morning yoga on my last day in Afghanistan. Eidie, the fat, cross-eyed cat, sat on our backs as we did downward-facing dog, then resumed his position on a cushion as our yoga master.

And, in the evening, my final meal. Shersha made Shersha Balls and his famous trifle and we played Settlers of Catan on cushions and rugs in the garden. Pancha lolled around with

Shazadah, lonely now that Perrito had gone to live with a colleague of Alex's. Pancha was my ideal dog. Perhaps more like a cat than a dog. She looked at me with her brown Afghan eyes and returned to Shazadah. Pancha knew that I was going. She knew that I would not return.

I couldn't sleep that night, of course. I lay on my monk's bed, my head rocking and plummeting with an Afghan rug of memories. Endlessly changing, never fully grasped.

The final morning. Wais came to collect me early and everyone stood at the gate. I couldn't comprehend what I was leaving and I think I never will. I felt like I had lived a whole life in Kabul. Shazadah cried, Shersha was stoic, Allegra and Jennifer were red-eyed as I patted Pancha for the last time. I hugged Shabheer tight. He didn't know it, but I was his brother.

Wais lifted my bags, viola and cello into the car and we left. Through the vice-president's checkpoints, past the soldiers with their teapot and rocket-propelled grenades, past the stray dogs and stray people, past ANIM and down Silo Road, past the blue street rocks of beggar women in burqas, past a father holding his son's shoulder as they walked, past a flock of sheep grazing by the road, past KFC (Kabul Fried Chicken), past paddling-pool sellers, past men waiting with carts for a day's work labouring, past open drains and newly paved roads, past dudes on motorbikes and officials in four-wheel drives, past countless bored soldiers with anger in their eyes, past children playing with a stick and tyre, past advertisements for 3.75G mobile plans, past cars with children sitting in the open boot, past young trees and rubble, past dusty and glorious roses, past everything, out towards the Hindu Kush.

Wais drove me to the outer parking lot and we sat together in his car. This huge, soft, wild man cried as I tried, in my simple Dari, to tell him how much I would miss him, how much he meant to me. And how grateful I was, because Wais had kept us all safe. He drove like a maniac partly because he was one, but also because it stopped us from being kidnapped. I told Wais he could have my motorbike. He hugged me and said thank you, but I knew that, for him, a motorbike didn't make up for my leaving. Because Wais loved us all.

So many times I had left Kabul and each time the security guards were aggressive and surly. This time I felt a power guide me through the airport, like a force field of happiness and certainty. I was waved through every checkpoint, surrendered to going through the female body-check line one last time and ended up at the flydubai desk, talking with Mohammad, a customs officer.

'Where are you going? You have many things.'

'I am going home to Australia. I worked here for a year. I am leaving Kabul.'

'Ah, Australia. My friends, they want to go to Australia. But why should I leave here and clean someone's dog in Australia? Here people respect me. I love my life. I am happy here.'

Finally, beyond Atesh and Laila, someone who wanted to stay. I entered the immigration queue and was asked for a bribe. Politely, mind you.

The final security check, and the officer saw my instruments.

'What is this?'

'This is a cello, and this is a viola. I teach music.'

The officer's eyes sparkled. 'So you know Afghan music?'

'Yes! I love Afghan music.'

'Please play us some!'

I took out my viola and played them the melody that Bibi Mina the trumpeter had played countless times in girls' ensemble, from a piece called 'Sultan-e-Qalba'. The officer joined in, his hands twirling in dance and his colleagues grinning. Security at Kabul Airport was some of the tightest in the world, but nowhere else in the world would you have a guard singing a love song with you.

Living in Afghanistan was like living inside a poem. It was always open to interpretation. And I would never understand.

∽

Carol was waiting for me in Dubai, calm, wise and bright. Over the next month we travelled to England and Scotland, slowly washing the dust of Kabul from my body and my mind. Loud noises still disturbed me and I became extremely anxious about security. I dreamt one night that all my fingers and thumbs had been hacked off and my hands left like two spoons.

It was time to go home.

On 21 July 2016 I lay face down on the examination table, my trousers pulled down a little. Dr Bearman drew up into her syringe a thick drug, suspended in castor oil. A drug that would release the man within. Testosterone.

The injection lasted about a minute, the drug going first into my gluteus maximus, then, over the next few weeks, slowly releasing into my bloodstream, changing every single atom in my body. I would need to take it every two months or so for the rest of my life.

As I lay there, breathing out the pain, my mother came into my head. I was born to her, for a still unknown reason, without my body having been properly exposed to testosterone. And now, after nearly fifty years, it would be. I felt myself go through the birth canal and out into the light. Finally, I had in my body what most people never have to think about—a chemical expression of their true selves. An infinite birthday present.

The day before, my last day of being chemically a woman, I had marvelled at how I had survived for so long. I had reflected about the years lost, having been born in a woman's body. But I was so glad that I had learnt what it is to be a woman in this world. And to experience the complexity and difficulties and glories of being seen as female.

I feel a great need to make up for lost time. I look now at cis (born) males and often wonder if they know the value of their gender and appreciate it. I hope I will appreciate being male. Every minute. And I am thankful for being able to see both sides and to choose the type of man I want to be.

Testosterone works its magic slowly. As I write this, it is six months since I began my treatment. The biggest change so far has been my voice, which has dropped an octave. It was not an easy process—for weeks I unconsciously held on to my old pitch, until it became too painful. I had vocal vertigo, afraid of falling. As I spoke, I anticipated a certain pitch to come out and a chaotic one did instead; it was as if someone had taken the strings of my cello and mixed them up. Curiously, and perhaps Freudianly, my voice finally relaxed one morning when I was speaking to my mother. I have grown more hair on my body and my face, my skin and jaw have thickened, my hips have thinned out, my muscles strengthened. I find a new, sometimes brutal logic in my thinking. But I can still, very happily, cry. As my oestrogen disappears and the man I am is slowly revealed, so is a profound contentment.

It will take up to five years for testosterone's changes to be complete. I have to be patient and understand that becoming the man I am takes time, like learning an instrument. I must also understand that I will never be the same as a cis man, but there is a great magic in that because we trans men are very special: men who have been inside the realm of women.

In the words of my friend Denise, 'It won't be simple, but it will be great.'

Transposition of anything takes time. Dr Sarmast surely knows this more than anyone, taking Western music and transposing it into Afghan society, taking Afghan society and transposing it back into the world he grew up in. And he also knows that everyone has the right to be who they are and to play the music they want.

The Afghanistan National Institute of Music remains one of the few successes of the last decade in Afghanistan. Afghan music has been brought back from the brink of extinction and Western instruments have been reintroduced into the school. Hundreds of children have been taken off the streets and introduced to a world of beauty, organisation and relative calm. They have played concerts around the world and learnt the most important thing any of us can learn: their own capability.

Would it have been better to only have Afghan instruments taught at the school? Did it make a difference to donors, seeing a young Afghan girl playing that most recognisable of Western instruments, the cello? Is that a Western-centric idea of the world? Would the money spent on Western teachers have been more useful in a dozen other schools, teaching more prosaic subjects? Was effective pedagogy put aside in the preparation for performances at Carnegie Hall to appease the American public?

And what of the sustainability of the school? Just after I left, the last remaining junior staff from their year, Masjedi and Sameem, left for Turkey. Dr Sarmast started again with the following year of graduates. And, if necessary, he shall start again with the year after that. Perhaps the changes in Afghanistan will happen, but as slowly as water changes a rock.

What about the moral state of the country and the school within it? At least one of the senior classes cheated on their final exams by taking a copy of the exam sheet from a teacher's computer; they were not dismissed from the school but given a new exam. The lack of accountability went on from year to year, teacher to student, parent to child.

And what of the people who decide to stay? How will they survive the constant corruption, nepotism, inertia? One graduate from ANIM, Samiullah, decided to stay. He won a scholarship at the American University of Kabul and had just begun his classes when the Taliban attacked the compound. Samiullah was killed.

Should these Afghans accept being born into this brutal place?

Should I have accepted being born in a woman's body?

And what of my own time at ANIM? I see now that I gained more than I gave. I gained a profound self-knowledge and acceptance, but I also believe, being a little kind to myself, that I gave many students skills to teach themselves, a thirst for greater knowledge and the sad understanding that most foreigners are temporary in their land.

During my year in Kabul there were dozens of attacks and hundreds of people died in the city alone. Yet four little children became cellists, four became viola players, five new double-bass players came into the world, four baby string quartets were formed, a chamber orchestra was born and countless concerts were given. And surely that was worth any cost.

I wrote this book because I didn't want people to only read yet another glossy magazine article about ANIM. I wanted to show how these kids are, in so many ways, like kids all over the world. I wanted to show what they have to deal with and how their challenges and, yes, their failures make their successes even more glorious. And I wanted you, dear reader, to know the true challenges and therefore the true courage of Dr Sarmast.

Epilogue

Destiny is a saddled donkey; he goes wherever you lead him.

PASHTUN PROVERB

Everyone's lives continued to follow their own paths, as the earth continues to spin, the roses to bloom, soldiers to battle.

The babies still play their instruments and new violin and cello teachers eventually came to ANIM. The girls' ensemble (renamed the Ensemble Zohra), including darling Meena, little Cevinch, rosy-cheeked Negin, poetic Shaperai, supermodel Nazira and green-eyed Marjan, performed at the World Economic Forum in Davos in January 2017.

Laila was given a visa to go to the Yale summer school. She returned to Kabul and is determined to study as an undergraduate at Yale. She applied for 2017 but was turned down. She will apply again. And, if necessary, again.

Hafizah spent some time away from school due to ill health, but eventually returned. She is becoming an excellent conductor and continues to help with the babies. For better or worse, she will always be the mother student.

Yalda returned to school and continues to study, although her back injury makes it very painful to sit for long periods. It is her hope that she will be offered a scholarship and be able to leave Afghanistan.

Jennifer and Alex moved to Bangkok, where Jennifer is taking a Masters in International Development. She receives As in every class.

Shabheer was granted his visa and he and Allegra left Kabul, as hoped, in August 2016. They have settled in Colorado. Allegra won a job as orchestra director at a prestigious school and Shabheer is making plans to start his own business.

Cami returned to Bogotá and is teaching and performing while he waits for his US residency to be approved. He then plans to move to Colorado and start a family with his wife.

Shersha and Shazadah stayed working at the Colombian House, now with three more foreign teachers. Shazadah returns to his village often, still their 'film-star boy'. Shersha's son Bilal spent time in hospital for his mental health and Shersha continues to make trifle.

Baset raised enough money and in August 2016 took up his place at Interlochen Center for the Arts in Michigan.

Milad and Fayez had their request for asylum approved. They stayed in New York and Milad had one of his pieces performed by the New York Philharmonic Chamber Orchestra, with him playing percussion. He is the first ever Afghan to play with the New York Philharmonic.

Shaheer made his way to Denmark, where he lives in a refugee camp. The possibility remains that he will be forcibly returned to Afghanistan.

Sama won a scholarship to study for a Masters in Business Management in India. She plans to return to Kabul, and she will keep her word.

Parwana is engaged to be married. Unlike Sama, it is what she always wanted.

Wais eventually left ANIM; he never developed the same friendship with the new foreign teachers as he had with us. He is working as a taxi driver and general dude around Kabul. Wais will always find a way through traffic and a way through the world.

Four of Farkhunda's murderers were sentenced to death and eight others given long prison sentences, including the mullah who made the original accusations. Eleven police officers were sentenced to a year in jail for not protecting Farkhunda. A few months later, an appeals court reduced all the death sentences to prison sentences. A panel of lawyers recommended the killers be retried. A trial date is yet to be set.

Pancha went to live with a friend of Jennifer's and killed his kitten. An Afghan to her core. She moved in with yet another friend who runs a Cambodian restaurant (yes, you read that correctly). I think about her every time I see another dog. Pancha was perfect.

And Atesh. That green-eyed puppy, he is nearly a man. He remains at ANIM, soaking in everything he can to make himself a better musician. I write to him regularly. Atesh always said that he never wanted to leave Afghanistan, but he has now changed his mind. I dream of him coming to Australia, to realise the musician that is within him.

Dr Sarmast still leads ANIM. He continues to be Afghanistan's musical warlord.

～

Afghanistan is slowly fading for me. My only glimpses of Afghanistan now are at a restaurant or in a news report or a snatch of music.

Afghanistan is a mirror. It shows you who you truly are. I miss it every day, but I know now that it is all right to love somewhere and leave it. We all have our own path and must follow it, at our peril. Leaving Kabul was like leaving the best bits of me behind, bits I had just found. Now I'll have to look for them in a new place.

When foreigners depart from Afghanistan they often leave behind a few possessions in silver aluminium boxes, hoping they may return, but knowing in their heart they never will.

In my silver box, I left Emma.

In memory of the missing girls

Playlist

The following is a list of the music I played, taught and listened to during my time in Kabul. I hope you gain as much pleasure and salve from it as I did.

Twinkle, Twinkle, Little Star—Suzuki Variations
Coriolan Overture—Beethoven
Quartet Op. 18 No. 1, slow movement—Beethoven
Turkish March—Mozart
Afghan music—Ay Shakhe Gul, Po Loyo Ghro Bande, Laili Jan,
    Sultan-e-Qalban, anything by Ahmad Zahir
Ode to Joy—Beethoven
Wooden Ships—Nigel Westlake
Mi Tierra—Gloria Estefan
Bizarre Fruit—M People
Speigel im Speigel—Arvo Pärt
Spem in Alium—Thomas Tallis
Du Shtetl À New York—Sirba Octet

In C—Terry Riley

Sailor's Dance—Glinka

I Have a Dream, Mamma Mia—ABBA

Symphony No. 5 and 6—Mahler

Cello Suite No. 1—J.S. Bach

Viola Sonata Op. 25 No. 1—Hindemith

I Got Rhythm—Cole Porter

Air on a G String—J.S. Bach

Anything by Destiny's Child, Joni Mitchell, Jason Isbell or
    Jacques Loussier—really, it's all amazing

Trumpet Concerto—Aritunian

Afghanistan Children's Anthem, Women's Song—Ustad Shefta

National Anthem of the Islamic Republic of Afghanistan—
    Babrak Wassa

My Heart Will Go On—Céline Dion

Waltz—Amy Beach

The Stars and Stripes Forever—Sousa

And finally, Voces8's *Eventide* album, especially John Williams'
    Hymn to the Fallen—most of this book was written to
    this album

Acknowledgements

Thank you:

To everyone at Allen & Unwin, especially Annette Barlow, Christa Munns and Simone Ford, for your kindness, encouragement and sensitivity.

To Richard Smart, for suggesting I write a book so many years ago, and helping me to find my voice. And for being there.

To John, Jo, Liz and Craggs, for giving so much to ANIM and to me. Your friendship is deeply treasured.

To all the other donors who helped buy the string instruments for ANIM. Your gift of music will live the longest.

To Hywel Sims and everyone at Musica Viva, for organising a special fund for the donations.

To Sydney Strings, for supplying the ANIM instruments and packing them so they survived the Kabul winter and the customs officers.

To Lauren, for help with research.

To Joan, Helen Therese, Gaye, Lyn and Rosie. Friends always.

To my doctors—Dr Bearman, Dr Saylor, Dr Bersin, Dr Margarian, Dr Toddhunter—for your care, intelligence, wit and professionalism. And to Dr Bearman for giving me the phrase 'Darwinianly robust', in reference to my ovaries.

To the Pattersons, for your love, jokes and cakes. Let's have another Uber evening!

To Mary and Emily Philip, for reading *Danger Music* and giving your suggestion of a playlist.

To Shireen Sandhu, for Australian red wine in Kabul, and for reading the first draft.

To Andrew Quilty, for your photographs, bewildering balance ability and manly hugs.

To Belinda and Celia, for opening your musical world to me.

To the Mexicans, Jennifer and Cami. Always together, no matter how far apart. Bring the whisky!

To Allegra Jan and Shabheer. You taught me not only how to live in Kabul, but how to thrive.

To the musicians of Afghanistan. You are the bravest people I will ever meet.

To my family. My love for you knows no limits.

And to Carol, my lion. My perfect partner. Ease, Joy and Glory. Thank you.

A portion of the profits from *Danger Music* will be used to support ANIM students studying overseas.